GRADING TERMS

A "good" coin is so worn that most of the detail has disappeared. These are not featured: only very rare specimens have any value.

FINE — A coin worn by considerable use, but still retaining clear lettering and some of the finer detail (hair, for example, not just a 'parting').

V.F. — The highest parts of a VERY FINE coin will show signs of its having been circulated. It must, however, possess a pleasing appearance devoid of disfiguring marks.

E.F. — An EXTREMELY FINE coin is almost perfect; close examination revealing traces of wear to the highest parts.

Unc. — UNCIRCULATED - unworn, as struck by the mint.

PROOF — is not a measure of condition, but a description of the method of manufacture. Certain exceptions apart; the field ("unprinted" part) will possess a mirror-like polish; the inscription, legend, or other design, will have a "frosted" appearance; the whole having an effect of great beauty which the smallest scratch will impair.

Excepting rare coins, the value of which is determined by the fact that nothing better is available, to be "collectable" a coin should possess (at least) the requirements of FINE given above. The 'head' should not be worn to a silhouette. The grading should never be qualified by "for its age": a FINE coin of 1800 should be no more worn than a FINE one of 1900 despite the hundred years age difference. The presence of ALL THE ORIGINAL DETAIL but with the highest parts barely flattened (new but 'shop-soiled') would be considered EXTREMELY FINE. Even uncirculated specimens will vie for honours according to freedom from mint bag-marks, brilliance etc., until the rare title of F.D.C. (fleur de coin) is awarded.

MARKETING

It is generally accepted that for the majority of coins a dealer's buying price is about 50% of his/her selling price. The dealer, in effect, is out-of-pocket until a buyer is found. A different 'deal' can be made where the coin is much sought after, particularly if the dealer has a customer in mind. Auction houses attract groups of buyers: collectors and dealers. Advertising, as you would to sell any other commodity, should stress any variety e.g. Obv.3 + Rev.B rather than a bare coin-date-condition.

CLEANING and POLISHING

A dealer's or auctioneer's list will sometimes indicate that a coin has been cleaned; a lower price results: the lesson should be clear. Cleaning diminishes value; polishing will TOTALLY DESTROY.

V.A.T. REGULATIONS: all coins less than 100 years old, whether or not they are legal tender, when supplied by VAT registered persons, are taxable at the present Standard Rate.

from 1760 in rising order of face-value

QUARTER-FARTHINGS to CROWNS
DECIMAL CENT to FIVE POUNDS

Copper, Bronze, Silver, Nickel-brass and Cupro-nickel

EVERY non-gold coin from 1760 separately listed for:

GEORGE III	House of HANOVER	1760 - 1820
GEORGE IV	House of HANOVER	1820 - 1830
WILLIAM IV	House of HANOVER	1830 - 1837
VICTORIA	House of HANOVER	1837 - 1901
EDWARD VII	SAXE-COBURG	1901 - 1910
GEORGE V	House of WINDSOR	1910 - 1936
EDWARD VIII	House of WINDSOR	1936
GEORGE VI	House of WINDSOR	1936 - 1952
ELIZABETH II	House of WINDSOR	1952 to date

Over TWO HUNDRED YEARS and NINE REIGNS

Photographs of coins, and information extracted from its reports, are reproduced with the permission of the Royal Mint.

A compilation of averaged selling-prices drawn from dealers' lists, auctions and numismatic magazines by

R. J. Marles for:

ROTOGRAPHIC PUBLICATIONS - 37 St. Efrides Road
Torquay - TQ2 5SG - ENGLAND

Copyright Registered at Stationers' Hall

Date	Mintage		Fine	V.F.	E.F.	abt Unc/FDC

VICTORIA   YOUNG HEAD   COPPER

Date	Mintage		Fine	V.F.	E.F.	abt Unc/FDC
1839	3,840,000		£2	£9	£25	£40/£60
1851			£3	£12	£30	£45/£75
1852	2,215,000		£2	£9	£18	£30/£45
1853			£4	£12	£24	£50/£75
1853	Proofs		(from the sets)	---		£200
1853	Cupro-nickel proofs		(P1615)	---		£260
1868	Bronze proofs		(P1616)	---		£200

THIRD FARTHINGS   FOR USE IN MALTA

GEORGE IV   COPPER

Date			Fine	V.F.	E.F.	
1827			£2	£4	£15	£40/£55
1827	Proof		---	--	£45	£175/£200

WILLIAM IV   COPPER

Date			Fine	V.F.	E.F.	
1835			£2	£4	£12	£30/£45
1835	noted (Seaby 1990)		GEF much lustre £25			---/---
1835	Proof		---	---	£160	---/---

VICTORIA   YOUNG HEAD

Date			Fine	V.F.	E.F.	
1844	1,301,040 COPPER		£3	£10	£30	£45/£60
1844	RE (for REG)		(P1607)	---	£225	£300/£400
1844	Large 'G'		---	£12	£40	£55/£95

"BUN" HEAD

Date			Fine	V.F.	E.F.	
1866	576,000 BRONZE		£1	£3	£6	£18/£25
1868	144,000 "		£1	£3	£8	£20/£30
1876	162,000 "		£1	£3	£9	£26/£40
1878	288,000 "		£1	£3	£9	£21/£30
1881	144,000 "		£1	£3	£8	£26/£35
1884	144,000 "		£1	£3	£8	£18/£25
1885	288,000 "		£1	£3	£8	£18/£25

Proofs: 1866 £135; 1868, 1876, 1881 rarely seen.

EDWARD VII   BRONZE

Date			Fine	V.F.	E.F.	
1902	288,000		---	£2	£4	£8/£12
1902	noted (Seaby 1990)		---	---	abt Unc £6	

GEORGE V   BRONZE

Date			Fine	V.F.	E.F.	
1913	288,000		---	£2	£4	£6/£12

HALF FARTHINGS   FOR USE IN CEYLON

GEORGE IV LAUREATE HEAD   COPPER

Date	Mintage		Fine	V.F.	E.F.	
1828	7,680,000 Rev A		£3	£7	£30	£60/----
1828	Rev B see below		£10	£30	£75	£150/£250
1830	8,776,320		£2	£12	£30	£50/£75
1830	Smaller date		£3	£16	£50	-.-/----
1830	Rev B see below		£12	£40	£85	£175/----

A number of proofs occur but no transactions noted.
Rev A: trident reaches above base of letters
Rev B: the trident reaches base of letters

Date	Mintage		Fine	V.F.	E.F.	Unc/abt. FDC.

WILLIAM IV   COPPER

Date	Mintage		Fine	V.F.	E.F.	Unc/abt. FDC.
1837	1,935,360		£10	£32	£100	£150/£180
1837	Noted		(Seaby 1990) GVF £45			---/---

VICTORIA YOUNG HEAD   COPPER EXCEPT WHERE INDICATED

Date	Mintage		Fine	V.F.	E.F.	Unc/abt. FDC.
1839	2,042,880		---	£3	£10	£30/£45
1842			---	£3	£12	£35/£50
1843	3,440,640		---	£3	£6	£9/£18
1844	6,451,000		---	£2	£4	£9/£15
1844	E of REGINA over N		£3	£9	£18	£30/£60
1847	3,010,560		---	£3	£12	£25/£40
1851	Unknown P1597		£2	£5	£15	£30/£45
1851	1 struck over 5 (Noted 1993)		£15	---	£45/---	
1852	989,184		---	£5	£18	£30/£45
1853	955,224		£1	£6	£25	£45/£65
1854	677,376		£1	£7	£26	£42/---
1856	913,920 P1603		£1	£8	£30	£40/£65
1856	(Noted 1993)		"Superb BU full lustre"			£250
1856	Large date		£16	£36	(not in Peck)	
1868	Bronze proof P1605		---	---	---	---/£175
1868	Cupro-nickel proof		---	---	---	---/£250

Proofs 1839 £200; 1853 £200; 1853 bronze £200

GEORGE III LONDON MINT - DATE BELOW BRITANNIA

Date	Mintage	Peck No.	Fine	V.F.	E.F.	Unc/FDC
1771		P909	£8	£25	£80	£160/£250
1771	1st 7 struck over 1			(1993)	"BU full lustre"	£295
1771	Proof	P910	---	---	---	£350/£500
1773		P911	£1	£5	£30	£60/£95
1773	No stop Rev.	P912	£6	£16	£40	£80/---
1773	Obverse 2	P913	£2	£10	£30	£60/---
1773	Obverse 2	P914	No stop Rev. £20	£30		£80/---
1773	No stop after Rex		£8	£25		on Peck 914
1774	Obverse 1	P915	£$	£12	£25	£60/£85
1774	Obverse 2	P916	£14	noted (1991)		
1775		P917	£3	£12	£40	£80/£120
1775	Inverted A for V	∀ in GEORGIVS	---	£65		---/---
1790	Pattern in silver	P1034	---	---	---	£650
1790	Pattern in copper	P1035	---	---	---	£450

SOHO (Birmingham) MINT - DATE BELOW BUST

Date	Mintage	Peck No.	Fine	V.F.	E.F.	Unc/FDC
1797	Pattern	P1199	---	---	---	£295
1797	Pattern	P1201	---	---	---	£225
1797	Pattern	P1202	---	---	---	£225
1798	Pattern	P1203	---	£95	---	£250
1798	Pattern	P1204	---	---	---	£220
1798	Pattern	P1212	---	---	---	£200
1798	Pattern	P1215	---	---	---	£280
1799	Three berries	P1279	£1	£3	£15	£25/£60
1799	Four berries	P1280	---	---	£70	£200/£350
1799	Proofs and Patterns abound, averaging				£150 to £250 FDC	
1799	Proof	P1390 bronzed		noted FDC		£90
1799	Proof but with groove as currency			GEF £45		---
1805	Pattern	P1319 bronzed		---	FDC	£275
1806	Portrait 1	P1396	---	£2	£10	£22/£45
1806	Portrait 2	P1397	£1	£3	£12	£25/£50
1806	Incuse dot	P1398	---	£20	£40	£80/£125
1807	Portrait 1	P1399	£3	£7	£15	£45/£85

Obverse 1 has row of breastplate scales, broken by rose at centre
Obverse 2 has a full, unbroken, row of eight scales

GEORGE IV Laureate Head DATE BELOW BRITANNIA

Date	Mintage	Peck No.	Fine	V.F.	E.F.	Unc/abt FDC
1821	2,688,000	P1407	£1	£3	£12	£20/£45
1821	G of GRATIA over O	(Coin Cooke mint state £69)				
1821	Proof in copper		---	---	---	£350/---
1822	5,924,352	P1409	50p	£2	£10	£20/£45
1822	Proof in copper		---	---	---	£350/---
1822	Obverse 2	P1411	50p	£2	£10	£40/£50
1823	2,365,440	P1412	£1	£3	£12	£25/£45
1823	Date has I for 1		£5	£16	£30	£60/£95
1825	4,300,800	Obv.1 P1414	£1	£2	£8	£24/£40
1825	5 over 3 (Noted 1993)		£25	---	£45	---/---
1825	D of DEI over U		£10	£40	£80	---/---
1825	Obverse 2	P1414A	£2	£6	£16	£28/£45
1825	Proof in gold	P1415	---	---	extremely rare	
1826	6,666,240	P1416	£1	£3	£15	£35/£50
1826	I for 1	noted	£80	---	---	£350/---

Undraped or Bare Head DATE BELOW HEAD

Date	Mintage	Peck No.	Fine	V.F.	E.F.	Unc/abt FDC
1826	Inc. above	P1439	£1	£3	£12	£45/£60
1826	Roman I for 1 in date	(1993)	"Choice uncirculated"			£200
1826	Bronzed Proof	P1440	---	---	£50	£95/£125
1826	Copper Proof	P1441	---	---	£60	---
1827	2,365,440	P1442	£2	£4	£18	£40/£65
1828	2,365,440	P1443	£2	£3	£12	£35/£60
1829	1,505,280	P1444	£3	£9	£30	£50/£95
1830	2,365,440	P1445	£2	£4	£15	£40/£80
1830	Noted 1993		---	---	"Superb"	£95

All dies are punched more than once. If one blow fails to register with another, then figures appear doubled, even trebled: this is very common. A major misalignment, however, will add value to the coin.

Obverse 1: Peck says 'the leaf-midribs (if present) are single raised lines'
Obverse 2: The 3 lowest leaves have incuse midribs.

Patterns V Proofs · If the currency which follows differs then the pattern remains as such. If, however, the currency is based on the pattern then the pattern becomes a proof of that currency. The pattern is a "loner", the proof has "friends".

FARTHINGS COPPER

Date	Mintage		Peck No.	Fine	V.F.	E.F.	abt. Unc/FDC

WILLIAM IV — DATE BELOW HEAD - 21mm

Date	Mintage		Peck No.	Fine	V.F.	E.F.	abt. Unc/FDC
1831	2,688,000		P1466	£1	£4	£16	£40/£60
1831	Proof		P1467	----	bronzed		£200/£300
1831	Proof		P1468	inverted	reverse		---/£150
1831	Proof		P1469	----	copper		---/£375
1834	1,935,360	Rev.A	P1470	£1	£4	£16	£30/£50
1834	Reverse B		P1471	£2	£5	£25	£60/£85
1835	1,720,320	Rev.A	P1472	£2	£7	£35	---/---
1835	Reverse B		P1473	£1	£4	£12	£30/£50
1836	1,290,240		P1474	£2	£5	£18	£50/£75
1837	3,010,560		P1475	£2	£5	£12	£45/£70

Reverse B has raised line down the arms of saltire (cross of St.Andrew); whereas A has incuse line

VICTORIA YOUNG HEAD — DATE BELOW HEAD - 21mm

Date	Mintage	Peck No.	Fine	V.F.	E.F.	abt. Unc/FDC
1838	591,360	P1553	£1.25	£3	£10	£30/£45
1838	DEF : on	P1553	£3	£6	£25	---/---
1839	4,300,800	P1554	£1	£3	£9	£20/£40
1839	Proofs in copper, some bronzed. Bronzed					---/£180
1839	Two pronged trident		---	£3	£9	£20/£65
1840	3,010,560	P1559	£1	£3	£12	£20/£40
1840	Variety on	P1559	DEF..	£3	£12	---/---
1841	1,720,320	P1560	£1	£3	£13	£18/£30
1841	Varieties P1560	REG.	and	REG for REG:		£20/£30
1841	Proof	P1561	If offered could fetch £800			
1842	1,290,240	P1562	£3	£7	£20	£45/---
1842	Variety on P1562		£5 large '42' in date			
1843	Struck over 1842		---	---	---	---/---
1843	4,085,760	P1563	£1	£3	£10	£20/£50
1843	I for 1 in date		£25	£50	£100	£200/---
1844	430,080	P1565	£15	£40	£200	£550
1845	3,225,600	P1566	£1	£3	£12	£25/£60
1845	Large date	F/GF	£45	(Colin Cooke 1991)		
1846	2,580,480	P1567	£2	£8	£32	£60/---
1847	3,879,720	P1568	£1	£3	£10	£20/£50
1847	Proof		You could get £1100 for yours!			
1848	1,290,246	P1569	£1	£4	£12	£25/£60
1849	645,120	P1570	£6	£21	£50	£200
1850	430,080	P1571	£1	£4	£14	£28/£42
1850	5 over inverted 5	5	---	---	---	---/---
	possibly, 5 over damaged 5 (no upright stroke) and much like a 3					
1850	5 over 4 Noted 1993		gEF		abtUNC £45	

HARINGTON and LENNOX farthing tokens are to be found in "Collectors' Coins: Ireland" (they feature the 'Irish' harp).
From James I to Charles I there were Richmond rounds - Transitional, Maltravers rounds, Richmond ovals and Maltravers ovals.

FARTHINGS

Date	Mintage	Peck No.	Fine	V.F.	E.F.	abt. Unc/FDC

VICTORIA YOUNG HEAD — COPPER · DATE BELOW HEAD · 21mm

Date	Mintage	Peck No.	Fine	V.F.	E.F.	abt. Unc/FDC
1851	1,935,360	P1572	£6	£15	£30	£60/£95
1851	D of DEI STRUCK OVER ▽		£200	£500	---	---/---
1852	822,528	P1574	£5	£15	£30	£65/£120
1853	1,028,628	P1575	30p	£1	£4	£16/£40
1853	3 struck over 2	--	--	--	---	£45/£70
1853	Proof, bronzed, with inverted reverse		---	---	---/---	
1853	Proof with raised W.W. P1577		---	---	£250/£350	
1853	WW incuse	P1578	£2	£6	£15	£25/£40
1853	Proof with incuse W WP1579		---	---	£200/£300	
1854	6,504,960	P1580	£1	£3.50	£10	£25/£50
1855	3,440,640	P1581 W W incuse	£11	£25	£45/£90	
1855	Included	P1582 W.W. raised	£11	£25	£45/£90	
1856	1,771,392	P1583	£3	£6	£20	£45/£90
1856★	R over E (VICTORIA) P1584		£15	£60	£100	£325/---
1856★	Noted 1992 "Fine/gdFine" £17			Mason World Coins		
1857	1,075,200	P1585	£1	£2.50	£10	£20/£40
1858	1,720,320	P1586	£1	£3	£8	£20/£35
1858	Small date		£10	£20	£40	---/---
1859	1,290,240	P1587	£5	£15	£50	£75/£125
1860	Obverse date currency		C. Cooke 1990 abt Unc £3900			
1860	Obverse date proof		C. Cooke 1990 abt Unc £3600			
1864	Noted 1993	P1589 Colin Cooke not selling even at £7,500!				

VICTORIA "BUN" HEAD BRONZE · DATE BELOW BRITANNIA · 20mm

BB = Border of Beads   TB = Toothed Border

Date	Mintage	Peck No.	Fine	V.F.	E.F.	abt. Unc/FDC
1860	2,867,200 with various "Berries-in-Wreath" obverses:					
1860	BB 3 berries	P1854	£1.50	£4	£8	£16/£24
1860	Proof	P1856	---	---	---	£175
1860	MULE combining beaded and toothed borders:					
		P1857	£100	£150	£250	---/---
1860	TB 4 berries	P1858	20p	£1	£4	£8/£20
1860	Bronze proof		---	---	---	£175
1860	TB 5 berries	P1859	20p	£1	£3	£7/£18
1860	Noted 1993	P1859	---	"Full lustre"		£25

★1856 Also described as E over R. Either R was struck over an incorrect E, or E was wrongly selected to improve a poor R. (or ?)

Date	Mintage	Peck	Fine	V.F.	E.F.	Unc/FDC
VICTORIA	(continued)	DATE BELOW BRITANNIA		- 20mm		
1861	8,601,600 4 berries	P1860	75p	£2	£8	£16/£24
1861	Bronze proof	(Cooke 1993)		choice	FDC	---/£165
1861	Obv. 3 (5 berries)		35p	£1.50	£5	£12/£20
1861	Date has small '8'		65p	£2.50	£4.50	£12/---
1862	14,336,000	P1865	50p	£1.80	£4	£12/£25
1862	Proof		---	---	£200	---/---
1862	Large 8 over small 8	(1990)			£30	---/---
1863	1,433,600	P1867	£10	£25	£50	£125/£250
1864	2,508,800	P1869	£1	£3	£6	£20/£40
1864	Angled horizontal bar to 4		---	£7	£12	£30/£50
1864	COPPER see P1589			Date Below Head on page 7		
1865	4,659,200	P1873	£1	£3.50	£8	£15/£30
1865	5 over 2	P1872A	£1	£3	£12	£25/£60
1865	5 over 3	---	£1	£4	£14	£20/£35
1865	Date has small '8'		£1.20	£3.75	£6.50	£15/---
1866	3,584,000	P1875 (D.Mason 1990)	75% lus.	£6		Full £30
1867	5,017,600	P1878	£1	£3	£8	£18/£35
1868	4,851,208	P1881	£1	£2	£6	£16/£24
1868	Bronze proof	P1882	---	---	---	£145/£250
1869	3,225,600	P1884	£1.25	£6	£15	£25/£55
1872	2,150,400	P1885	£1	£3	£6	£15/£30
1873	3,225,620	P1886	50p	£2	£5	£15/£25
1873	Low set 3 in date				£8	£16/£30
	Proofs also occur for 1861, 1862, 1863, 1866, 1867.					
	OBVERSE 4 'AGED' (MATRONLY) BUST - still 'BUN' HEAD					
	'H' (centred below date) = Heaton Mint					
1874H	3,584,000	P1887	45p	£2	£6	£12/£18
1874H	Bronze proof	(noted 1991)		about FDC		---/£170
1874H	Gs struck over ⊙ s		£50	£120	£240	£425/---
1875	712,760	P1890	£5	£10	£22	£55/---
1875	Large date	(5 berries)		£12	£25	£50/£90
1875	Small date	(5 berries)		£22	£45	£100/£300
1875	Small date	(4 berries)		£25	£50	£175/£350
1875H	6,092,800	P1892	25p	75p	£5	£10/£24
1876H	1,175,200	P1894	£4	£9	£25	£40/£96
1876	RF.G for REG		£5	---	---	---/---
1877	Proofs only	P1895	bronze	(Cooke '93)		£2350
1877	Bronzed proof			guesstimate		£1400/£1600
1878	4,008,540	P1896	25p	75p	£5	£10/£22
1878	Proof	P1897	---	---	---	--/£325
1879	3,977,180	P1898	25p	75p	£5	£10/£22
1879	Date has large '9'		£1	£4	£8	£12/£25
1880	1,842,710 4 berries	P1899	£1	£3	£9	£12/£25
1880	3 berries	P1901	£2	£20	£40	£60/£100
	Proofs, in bronze, for all except 1876H and 1879.					

The earliest legal farthings were made in 1613 under Royal Licence purchased from King James I by Lord Harington. 'Haringtons', and other Royal Farthings, have a harp reverse and the contraction 'HIB'. These are catalogued in "COLLECTORS COINS: IRELAND".

Date	Mintage	Peck	Fine	V.F.	E.F.	abt. Unc/FDC
VICTORIA	continued - mainly obverse 5 - BRONZE					
1881	See below	Obv.4 P1901	A £20	£30	£40	£80/£120
1881	3,494,670	Obv.5 P1902	50p	£2	£4	£9/£20
1881H	1,792,000	P1904	£1	£3	£6	£12/£22
1882H	1,792,000	P1905	75p	£2	£7	£14/---
1883	1,128,680	P1907	£2	£4	£16	£25/£40
1884	5,782,000	P1909	15p	50p	£1	£5/£15
1885	5,442,308	P1911	25p	£1	£2	£5/£15
1886	7,767,790	P1913	25p	£1	£2	£5/£15
1887	1,340,800	P1915	£1	£2	£7	£16/£30
1888	1,887,250	P1916	75p	£1	£5	£12/£25
1890	2,133,070	P1917	75p	£1	£5	£12/£25
1891	4,959,690	P1919	40p	£1	£4	£9/£15
1892	887,240	P1921	£3	£5	£10	£25/£40
1893	3,904,320	P1923	50p	£1	£4	£15/£25
1893	Narrower date		£1	£2	£5	£15/£25
1894	2,396,770	P1924	50p	£1	£6	£9/£18
1895	2,852,852	P1925	£3	£8	£20	£30/£60

Proofs occur except 1881H, 1887, 1888, 1893, 1895.

VICTORIA		'Old' or 'Widow' Head				
1895	Inc above	P1958	25p	£1	£4	£8/£16
1896	3,668,610	P1959	25p	£1	£3	£4/£8
1896	Noted		(Full lustre, quite exceptional)			£12.50
1897	4,579,800:		blackened to distinguish from half-sovereign			
1897	Undarkened	P1961	£1	£3	£10	£20/£35
1897 ★	Horizon as P1961 but black finish		---	---		£12/£18
1897 ★★	Higher horizon	P1962	25p	£1	£3	£5/£9
1898	4,010,080	P1963	25p	£1	£4	£8/£12
1899	3,864,616	P1964	25p	£1	£4	£8/£12
1900	5,969,317	P1965	25p	60p	£2	£4/£8
1901	8,016,459	P1966	15p	35p	£1	£2/£4

Proofs occur for 1896 and, possibly, for 1901.

Obverse 4 has 4 berries in wreath arranged as two pairs (2+2 and not 1+2+1 as previously). Obverse 5 has 3 berries arranged 2+1.
★   Rev A 7 points TO a border tooth
★★ Rev B 7 points BETWEEN two teeth

FARTHINGS

EDWARD VII

Date	Mintage		Fine	V.F.	E.F.	abt Unc./FDC
					BRONZE · 20mm	
1902	5,125,120		25p	£1	£2	£4/£9
1903 ★	5,331,200	★ low horizon	30p	£1	£3	£9/£12
1904	3,628,800		75p	£2	£4	£9/£14
1905	4,076,800		25p	£1	£4	£9/£14
1906	5,340,160		25p	75p	£4	£9/£14
1907	4,399,360		25p	£1	£4	£9/£14
1908	4,264,960		20p	60p	£4	£9/£14
1909	8,852,480		20p	45p	£3	£10/£14
1910	2,598,400		£1.50	£3	£6	£14/£21

All chemically darkened to avoid confusion with gold.

FARTHINGS BRONZE · 20mm

GEORGE V   ALL DARKENED, CHEMICALLY, UNTIL 1918

Date	Mintage		Fine	V.F.	E.F.	abt. Unc./FDC
1911	5,196,800	(see foot of page) 25p	£1	£3.50	£6/£12
1912	7,669,760		40p	£1.50	£5/£7
1913	4,184,320		65p	£1.50	£5/£7
1914	6,126,988	BRITT obv 1	65p	£3	£9/£14
1914		BRIT T obv 2	65p	£3	£9/£14
1915		BRITT	£40	"Guesstimate"	---/---
1915	7,129,254	BRIT T	65p	£3	£5/£12
1915	Noted 1993		---	"Superb"	£16
1916	10,993,325		25p	£1	£3/£6
1917	21,434,844		15p	£1	£3/£4
1918	19,362,818	left bright	15p	£1	£2/£3
1918	Rare darkened finish		---	£6	£10/£15
1919	15,089,425		20p	£1	£2/£5
1920	11,480,536		20p	80p	£2/£5
1921	9,469,097		20p	80p	£2/£5
1922	9,956,983		20p	£1	£3/£6
1923	8,034,457		25p	£1	£3/£5
1924	8,733,414		25p	£1	£3/£6
1925	12,634,697		20p	£1	£3/£5
1926	9,792,397		20p	75p	£3/£6
1927	7,868,355		15p	50p	£2/£4
1928	11,625,600		15p	75p	£2/£3.50
1929	8,419,200		15p	75p	£2/£4
1930	4,195,200		15p	£1	£2/£4
1931	6,595,200		15p	£1	£2/£5.50
1931	Bronze proof	(Peck 2347)	---	---	/£165
1932	9,292,800		15p	50p	£2/£3
1932	Bronze proof	Noted 1993	"A super FDC"		/£163
1933	4,560,000		20p	£1	£2/£5
1933	Proof	(Peck 2353) (1993)	---	---	£195
1934	3,052,800		25p	£1.50	£4/£7
1934	Proof	(Peck 2355) (1993)	"Stunning FDC"		£195
1935	2,227,200		65p	£3	£6/£15
1936	9,734,400	★ issued posthumously	15p	25p	£1/£2.50

'Fine' are sold, usually from 'The Tray' 5p to 25p

EDWARD VIII   Duke of Windsor

1937   Extremely rare - not issued for general circulation.

GEORGE V
1911   The 'standard' Peck obverse 1 has two variations:
Obverse 1a = above B.M. the neck is hollow.
Obverse 1b = above B.M. the neck is flat.
At present, values are identical even amongst dealers who
DO distinguish the variety - many don't; but more are doing so.

Date	Details	Peck No.	V.F.	E.F.	abt. Unc/FDC/FDC
GEORGE VI					
1937	8,131,200	---	---	40p	£1/ £2/ ---
1937	26,402 proofs	---	---	---	£3/ £4/ £6
1938	7,449,600	---	20p	50p	£3/ £6/ ---
1939	31,440,000	---	---	15p	45p/90p/ ---
1940	18,360,000	---	---	25p	80p/ £1/ £2
1941	27,312,000	---	---	20p	60p/95p/ ---
1942	28,857,600	---	---	20p	75p/ £1/ ---
1943	33,345,600	---	---	20p	60p/95p/ ---
1944	25,137,600	---	---	15p	45p/65p/ ---
1945	23,736,000	---	---	15p	45p/65p/ ---
1946	23,364,800	---	---	15p	60p/90p/ ---
1946	Bronze proof (1991) P2476 (possibly 3 only)				£225
1947	14,745,600	---	---	15p	60p/90p/ ---
1948	16,622,400	---	---	15p	60p/90p/ ---
1949	8,424,000	---	---	20p	75p/ £2/ ---
1949	Bronze proof (1994) "One of possibly 3 or 4"				£225
1950	10,324,800	---	---	15p	40p/75p/ ---
1950	17,513 proofs	---	---	---	£3/ £5/ £7
1951	14,016,000	---	---	---	40p/60p/75p
1951	20,000 proofs	---	---	---	£4/ £5/ £6
1952	5,251,200	---	---	15p	60p/90p/ ---
1952	Bronze proof P2488	---	---		£125/£175/ ---
1952	Bronze proof Noted 1993 "Choice FDC, excessively rare"				£225

ELIZABETH II

Date	Details	Peck No.	V.F.	E.F.	abt. Unc/FDC/FDC
1953	6,131,037 :				
1953	Obv.1 Rev. A P2520 Currency Set				50p/ £1/£1.50
1953	Obv.1 Rev. B P2520A	---	---		£10/£20/ ---
1953	Obv.2 Rev. A P2520B	---	---		£15/£25/£35
1953	Obv.2 Rev. B P2521	---	---	10p	40p/75p/ £1
1953	40,000 proofs P2522 (of P2521)	---			£2/ £4/ £6
1953	Proofs 2 + A				£40/£60/£80
1954	6,566,400	---	---	15p	25p/35p/80p
1955	5,779,200	---	---	20p	30p/65p/ ---
1956	1,996,800	---	---	30p	50p/75p/ ---

Obverse 1 is poorly defined · the cross points TO a border bead.
Obverse 2 is sharper · the cross points BETWEEN two border beads.
Reverse A (dies of George VI) · 'F' points BETWEEN two beads.
Reverse B is similar but the 'F' points TO a border bead.

1953 Obverse/Reverse Rarity Scale 1 + A (C) 2 + A (R)
1 + B (R) 2 + B (VC)
(R) = Rare · (C) = Common · (VC) = Very Common

Date	Details	Fine	V.F.	E.F.	abt. Unc/FDC
GEORGE III *Tower - London - Mint* COPPER 29 mm					
1770	Armoured Bust	£2	£10	£45	£85/£150
1770	No stop reverse P893A	---	---	---	---
1770	P894 and P895		Proofs in silver, and in copper		
1771	P896	£2	£10	£45	£70/£110
1771	P897 no stop reverse	---	£10	£45	£90/£130
1771	P898 ball below spear head		---	£40	£80/£120
1772	P899 and P902	£2	£10	£50	£90/£140
1772	P900 GEORIVS (error)	£4	£15	£50	£110/£160
1772	P901 ball below spear head		---	£40	£80/£120
1772	P903 no stop reverse	---	£10	£45	£90/£130
1773	P904	£2	£9	£30	£60/£90
1773	P905 no stop after REX	---	£9	£40	£80/£120
1773	P906 no stop reverse	---	£12	£50	£90/£140
1774	P907	£3	£12	£35	£65/£100
1775	P908	£3	£14	£45	£85/£130
1775	Noted 1993 (K.B.Coins) "Superb Mint State"				£175
1788	P966 Gilt proof	---	---	---	£195
1795	P1044 Cartwheel Pattern		(abtEF £99 1989) ---		

Soho - Birmingham - Mint

DATE BELOW BRITANNIA					COPPER 30 mm
1797	Pattern P1154	---	£135	(1988)	
1799	Gilt proof P1156	---	---	---	FDC £340
1799	Bronzed proof P1234	---	---	---	FDC £90
1799	Bronzed proof P1247	---	---	---	£110/---
1799	5 incuse gunports P1248	£1	£3	£20	£40/£60
1799	6 raised gunports P1249	£1	£3	£15	£25/£45
1799	Plain hull P1251	£1	£5	£20	£40/£60
1799	9 raised gunports P1250	£1	£4	£18	£38/£55
1799	Raised line, no gunports P1252	£5		£20	£45/£60

DATE BELOW HEAD					COPPER 29 mm
1805	Pattern by Taylor · Noted 1993 "Virtually As Struck"				£175
1806	Olive branch, no berries	---	£2	£10	£40/£65
1806	Proofs, 'plain' and gilt (1993) "F.D.C."				£165
1806	3 berries, Soho underlined	---	£3	£12	£42/£68
1807	3 berries etc.	£1	£4	£16	£45/£70

SOHO MINT halfpennies have an edge milled in a deep groove; this gives the appearance of two halfpennies joined together.

GEORGE IV — LAUREATE HEAD — COPPER 28mm

Date	Mintage	Fine	V.F.	E.F.	Unc/FDC
1825	215,040	£4	£16	£35	£50/£85
1825	Proof	--	---	---	---/£150
1826	9,031,630 Rev A	£2	£6	£30	£45/£75
1826	Rev B	--	£8	£40	£75/£105
1826	Proof Rev B	--	--	£75	£100/---
1827	5,376,000	£1	£4	£35	£60/£95

Rev A; Saltire of shield has two incuse lines P1433
Rev B; Saltire of shield has one raised line P1436

WILLIAM IV — BARE HEAD — COPPER 28mm

Date	Mintage	Fine	V.F.	E.F.	Unc/FDC
1831	806,400	£1.25	£6	£30	£95/£125
1831	Proofs, bronzed	---	---	---	£95/---
1834	537,600	£1.25	£6	£30	£95/£125
1837	349,400	£1	£5	£20	£60/£90

VICTORIA Young Head — DATE BELOW HEAD — COPPER

Date	Mintage	Fine	V.F.	E.F.	Unc/FDC
1838	456,960	50p	£2	£15	£45/£65
1839	Proofs, bronzed	---	---	---	£80/---
1839	Proofs, bronzed, inverted reverse	---	---	---	£120/£150
1841	1,075,200	50p	£2	£12	£25/£45
1841	Proofs, bronzed	---	---	---	£90/---
1843	967,680	£3	£10	£35	£90/£130
1844	1,075,200	£1	£4	£25	£60/£85
1845	1,075,200	£16	£45	£160	£225/£375
1846	860,160	£2	£5	£25	£65/£90
1847	752,640	£2	£5	£25	£65/£90
1848	322,560	£1	£5	£25	£65/£90
1848 ★	8 over 7	---	£3	£15	£45/£65
1848	8 struck over 3	---	£12	£30	---/---
1851	215,040 (no dots)	---	£4	£12	£40/£55
1851	Shield, 7 incuse dots	---	£4	£15	£65/---
1852	637,056 (no dots)	---	£4	£15	£60/£75
1852	Shield, 7 incuse dots	---	£4	£15	£60/£80
1853	1,559,040	45p	£2	£7	£20/£30
1853	3 over 2	£3	£9	£18	£25/£45
1853	Proofs, bronzed, inverted reverse	---	---	---	---/£200
1853	Copper proof (Colin Cooke 1993)				---/£150
1854	12,354,048 ?	£1	£2	£8	£20/£30
1855	1,455,837	£1	£2	£8	£30/£45
1856	1,942,080	£1	£4	£20	£40/£60
1857	1,182,720 (no dots)	---	---	£15	£45/---
1857	Shield, 7 incuse dots	---	£2	£10	£20/£30
1858	2,472,960	50p	£3	£14	£36/---
	noted		(Seaby 1989 GEF £15)		
1858	Smaller date	£1	£3	£20	£46/---
1858	8 over 6	£2	£6	£15	£30/£50
1858	8 over 7	£1	£3	£9	£20/£30
1859	1,290,340	£1	£3	£14	£40/---
1859	9 struck over 8	£2	£6	£25	£45/---
1860 ★★	Extremely rare	£175	£500	£2200	£4000/---
1860 ★★	Extremely rare Proof	(1988)		EF+ £2700	----

★ Variety more common than correctly dated piece
★★ Date is below head, not below Britannia

VICTORIA "Bun" Head — DATE BELOW BRITANNIA

Date	Mintage	Fine	V.F.	E.F.	Unc/FDC
TYPE 1: BEADED BORDERS :					
1860	1 + A (P1750)	--	£2	£12	£20/£40
	noted (Seaby 1990 EF some lustre £16)			---	
	noted (Cooke 1993) "BU full lustre"				£34
1860	1 + A (P1751/52/53) Proofs bronze and bronzed				

TYPE 2: TOOTHED BORDERS :
Obv 2 has 7 berries. Obv 3 has 4 berries, all leaves have raised mid-ribs.
Obv 4 has 4 berries, but four leaves have double incuse lines to mid-ribs.
Lighthouse : B tapering, pointed   C cylindrical with rounded top.

Date	Mintage	Fine	V.F.	E.F.	Unc/FDC
1860	2 + B (P1754)	--	£2	£12	£25/£40
1860	3 + B (P1756)	--	£3	£15	£40/£60
1860	3 + C (P1757)	--	£3	£15	£40/£55
1860	4 + B (P1758)	£2	£6	£18	£50/£75
1860★	F of HALF struck over P (The Rawcliffe Halfpenny)				
		--	£60 (£25 1987)		---/---
1861	54,118,400 Ten obv/rev combinations + proofs				
1861	Without signature	50p	£2	£10	£15/£25
1861	Signature on rock	£1	£3	£20	£45/£65

★ FARTHINGS of this date bear Fs with little or no lower serif to the lower horizontal bar (illustr.) Perhaps the first halfpennies were struck with the same, or a similar, type-face and, to avoid having HALF PENNYs as well as FARTHINGS were overstruck.

Date below HEAD   Date below BRITANNIA

HALFPENNIES

Date	Mintage		Fine	V.F.	E.F.	Unc/FDC
VICTORIA	**DATE BELOW BRITANNIA**				**BRONZE 26 mm**	
1862	61,107,200:					
	L.C.W. on rock		£1	£3	£10	£20/£30
1862	Proof	P1775	--	--	---	£200
1862	No L.C.W.	P1776	--	£2	£8	£15/£25
1862	Proof	P1777	--	---	£200	
1862	A, B, or C to left of lighthouse					£360/£500
1862	Unbarred A l.e Λ	£120	---	---	--- / ---	
1863	15,948,800		75p	£2	£12	£30/£45
1864	537,600		£2	£5	£20	£35/£50
1865	8,064,000		£2	£5	£20	£35/£50
1865	5 over 3		£12	£50	£140	£265/£400
1866	2,508,800		£1	£4	£15	£25/£36
1867	2,508,806		£2	£5	£20	£36/£55
1868	3,046,400		£1	£4	£24	£36/---
1868	Cupro-nickel proof Noted 1993		(KB Coins)		"FDC"	£325
1869	3,225,600		--	£4	£20	£60/£95
1870	4,350,739		£1	£4	£24	£36/---
1871	1,075,280 ?		£12	£30	£85	£150/---
1872	4,659,410		£1	£4	£24	£36/---
1873	3,404,880		£1	£5	£25	£40/---
1874	1,347,665		£3	£14	£50	£85/---
1874	Portrait as 1874H		£1	£4	£24	£36/---
1874H	5,017,600		£1	£4	£20	£32/---
1874H	Proof		Noted 1993 (Cooke)		"FDC"	£150
1875	5,430,815		65p	£2	£16	£25/---
1875H	1,254,400		£2	£6	£25	£40/---
1876H	6,809,600		65p	£2	£16	£25/£45
1877	5,209,505		65p	£2	£16	£25/£45
1878	1,425,535		£2	£12	£36	£70/£140
1879	3,582,545		60p	£2	£12	£20/---
1880	2,423,465		£1	£5	£20	£30/£45
1881	2,007,515		£1	£5	£20	£30/£45
1881H	1,792,000		75p	£3	£15	£20/£35
1882H	4,480,000		75p	£3	£15	£20/£35
1883	3,000,725		75p	£4	£20	£28/---
1884	6,989,580		60p	£2	£12	£24/---
1885	8,600,574		60p	£2	£12	£24/£40
1886	8,586,155		50p	£2	£10	£20/£30
1887	10,701,305		50p	£1	£9	£20/£32
1888	6,814,070		35p	£1	£12	£18/---
1889	7,748,234		35p	£2	£12	£18/---
1889	9 over 8		£4	£20	£45	£90/---
1890	11,254,235		40p	£2	£10	£20/£30
1891	13,192,260		40p	£2	£10	£16/£25
1892	2,478,335		£1	£2	£10	£16/£25
1893	7,229,344		40p	£2	£9	£16/£25
1894	1,767,635		75p	£3	£10	£24/£36

Date	Mintage		Fine	V.F.	E.F.	Unc/abt FDC
VICTORIA		**Veiled, Old, or Widow Head**				
1895	3,032,154	P1950	30p	£1	£4	£9/£18
1896	9,142,500	P1951	25p	90p	£3	£8/£12
1897	8,690,315	P1951A	30p	£1	£4	£10/£15
1897	Horizon higher	P1952	---	90p	£3	£8/£12
1898	8,595,180	P1953	35p	£1	£4	£10/£15
1899	12,108,001	P1954	20p	60p	£3	£7/£12
1900	13,805,190	P1955	---	60p	£2	£5/£9
1901	11,127,360	P1956	---	---	£2	£4/£6
EDWARD VII						
1902	13,672,960		---	---	£3	£7/£10
1902	LOW TIDE variety		£2	£8	£32	£50/£80
1903	11,450,880		---	£1	£5	£15/£21
1904	8,131,200		---	£2	£8	£20/£28
1905	10,124,800		---	£1	£5	£14/£22
1906	11,101,440		---	£1	£4	£8/£12
1907	16,849,280		---	£1	£4	£8/£12
1908	16,620,800		---	£1	£5	£18/£24
1909	8,279,040		---	£1.50	£8	£20/£28
1910	10,769,920		---	£1	£5	£10/£16

Proofs exist for 1902; they are very rare.

"LOW TIDE" VARIETY referred to above and on page 14 may be determined thus: if the horizon meets Britannia at the point, below the knee, where right and left legs cross; NORMAL tide is indicated. If, however, the horizon meets Britannia at a much lower point - nearer the hem of her drape - then a LOW TIDE variety has been detected.

GEORGE V — BRITANNIA REVERSE — BRONZE 26mm

Date	Mintage	Fine	V.F.	E.F.	Unc/abt. FDC
1911	12,570,880		£1	£3	£7/£10
1912	21,185,920		£1	£3	£7/£10
1913	17,476,480		£1	£5	£12/£18
1914	20,289,111		£1	£4	£9/£12
1915	21,563,040		£1	£4	£9/£12
1916	39,386,143		70p	£4	£7/£10
1917	38,245,436	---	60p	£3	£7/£10
1918	22,321,072	---	60p	£3	£7/£10
1919	28,104,001	---	60p	£3	£7/£10
1920	35,146,793	---	60p	£3	£7/£10
1921	28,027,293	---	60p	£2	£6/£10
1922	10,734,964	---	£1.25	£4	£8/£12
1923	12,266,282	---	65p	£4	£7/£10
1924	13,971,038	---	65p	£4	£8/£12
1925	12,216,123 Head as for 1924		90p	£5	£9/£15
1925	Modified Head as for 1926		£1.50	£8	£12/£20
1926	6,712,306	---	£1	£6	£10/£15
1927	15,589,622	---	55p	£3	£7/£10
	SMALLER HEAD:				
1928	20,935,200	---	40p	£2	£3/£6
1928	Proof	---	(Spink 1988)		--/£175
1929	25,680,000	---	30p	£2	£3/£6
1930	12,532,800	---	30p	£2	£3/£6
1931	16,137,600	---	30p	£2	£3/£6
1932	14,448,000	---	30p	£2	£3/£6
1933	10,560,000	---	30p	£2	£4/£7
1934	7,704,000	---	40p	£2.50	£4/£9
1935	12,180,000	---	30p	£2	£4/£8
1936	23,008,800	---	---	£1	£2/£4

1911 Obverse 1a - the neck is hollow
Obverse 1b - the neck is flat
(See note on page 6)

Proofs 1926 to 1936 inclusive: British Museum.
1912 A and B

1911 Some dies were punched with date close to line of exergue (segment containing date)

Small gap = Rev A
Clear gap = Rev B

Combinations:
1a + A   1a + B
1b + A   1b + B

HALFPENNIES

EDWARD VIII *(Duke of Windsor)* — Reverse GOLDEN HIND

Date	Mintage	Fine	V.F.	E.F.	Unc/abt. FDC
1937	Excessively rare				

GEORGE VI — Reverse GOLDEN HIND

Date	Mintage	Fine	V.F.	E.F.	Unc/abt. FDC
1937	24,504,000	---	---	65p	£1/£3
1937	26,402 proofs		---	---	£3/£5
1938	40,320,000	---	10p	£1	£2/£4
1938	Noted (D. Mason 1994) "BU 100% lustre"				--/£5
1939	28,924,800		10p	£1.50	£2/£4
1940	32,162,400		30p	£2	£3/£5
1941	45,120,000		5p	45p	£1/£3
1942	17,908,800		5p	45p	£1/£3
1943	76,200,000		10p	50p	£1/£3
1944	81,840,000		5p	45p	£1/£3
1945	57,000,000		5p	70p	£1.50/£3.50
1946	22,725,600		30p	£2	£2/£4
1947	21,266,400		10p	£1	£3/£4
1948	26,947,200	---	10p	45p	£1/£2
1949	24,744,000	---	10p	£1	£4/£6
1950	24,153,600	---	10p	45p	£2/£4
1950	17,513 proofs	---	---	---	£2.50/£4
1951	14,868,000	---	20p	£1.20	£4/£6
1951	20,000 proofs	---	---	---	£2.50/£4
1952	33,278,400	---	10p	25p	50p/£2

1940
L *P* = Rev A
L *P* = Rev B
*L = Rev C
See 'pointings' page 32

ELIZABETH II

Cross points BETWEEN rim beads = Obverse 1
Cross points TO a rim bead = Obverse 2

Date	Mintage	Fine	V.F.	E.F.	Unc/abt. FDC
1953	8,910,000:				
1953	Obverse 1	---	---	---	£2.50
1953	Obverse 2	---	10p	20p	50p/£1
1953	40,000 proofs	---	---	---	£3
1954	19,375,200	---	10p	£1	£3/£4
1955	18,465,600	---	10p	£1	£2/£3
1956	21,799,200	---	---	£1	£3/£4
1957	39,672,000	---	---	20p	£1/£2
1957	Variety has a calm sea	---	---	£2	£6.50
1958	66,331,200	---	---	---	50p
1958	Proof Noted 1994	---	---	---	---/£75
1959	79,176,000	---	---	---	25p/75p
1960	41,340,000	---	---	---	30p/90p
1961	Decimal Patterns see page 88		---	---	---
1962	41,779,200	---	---	---	15p/50p
1963	42,720,000	---	---	---	10p/40p
1964	78,583,200	---	---	---	10p/25p
1965	98,083,200	---	---	---	10p/25p
1966	95,289,600	---	---	---	5p/15p
1967	146,490,400 Narrow rim	---	---	---	5p/15p
1967	Noted 1994 Wide rim (KB Coins)			"BU"	£2.50
	Total for 1967 includes 46,226,400 struck in 1968				
1970	750,424 LAST STERLING Proofs (1971/75)				£1

1925/27 Effigy modified to aid striking, all coins
1928 Smaller head, for halfpennies and pennies
1949 IND:IMP (Emperor of India) discontinued, all coins
1954 BRITT:OMN discontinued - all coins
1969 Halfpenny demonetized - 1st August

GEORGE III SOHO (Birmingham) MINT COPPER

DATE STRUCK INTO BROAD RIM 36mm THE "CARTWHEEL" PENNY

Date	Mintage	Fine	V.F.	E.F.	abt. Unc/FDC
1797	10 leaves in wreath	£4	£15	£50	£100/£150
1797	11 leaves in wreath	£4	£18	£60	£150/£200
1797	Bronzed proof	Auction (1988)			£175

DATE BELOW HEAD 34mm

Deep groove to edge suggests two joined coins:

1806	Incuse curl right of knot	- - -	£7	£25	£60/£100
1806	No incuse hair curl	(Seaby 1990)		GEF £65	
1806	P1325 Gilt proof (1994)	- - -	- - -	- - -	£135/£250
1806	P1327 Copper proof	- - -	- - -	- - -	£175
1806	P1328 Copper proof	- - -	- - -	- - -	£140/£250
1806	P1333 Bronzed proof (1990)	abt EF £50			- - - -/- - - -
1806	P1349 Copper re-strike proof	- - -	- - -	- - -	£160
1807	P1344	- - -	£7	£20	£30/£50
1808	One example known (Spink 1985)	- - -	- - -	- - - Mint	£15,000

Varieties, proofs, patterns; extensive.

DATE STRUCK INTO BROAD RIM 41mm "CARTWHEEL" TWOPENCE

1797	722,160	£5	£18	£60/£110	£200/£300
1797	Bronzed proofs (P1065)	- - -	- - -		£200/£300
1797	½d, ¼d, 1d, 2d set			£850	(Spink 1986)

These were the first coins (copper currency) to bear the initials D:G: (DEI GRATIA : "BY THE GRACE OF GOD"). Designed by Küchler, they were struck on steam powered presses installed by James Watt at the Soho, Birmingham, refineries of Matthew Boulton.

"8 of these shall weigh 1lb and measure one foot"

A break in the rising-face-value order has been made because this huge coin belongs with the very similar Küchler pennies. Weighing over 60 grams for each twopence, with 120 to the £1 (240 pence to £1), could you lift your weekly income if you were paid in Cartwheels?

PENNIES

GEORGE IV ROYAL (Tower) MINT COPPER 34mm

Date	Mintage	Fine	V.F.	E.F.	abt. Unc/FDC
1825	1,075,200 P1420	£3	£14	£45	£125/£170
1825	Proofs	- - -	- - -	- - -	£180
1826	5,913,000 P1422	£2	£10	£36	£95/£150
1826	St Andrew's Cross varieties:				
	Thin raised line		£12	£40	£100/£160
	Thick raised line		£16	£50	£120/£185
1826	Proofs: plain, varieties, bronzed	- - -	- - -	- - -	£100/£250
1827	1,451,520 Fair £15	£35	£85	£950	£1,500
1827	Noted (1991) GVF - no corrosion £290				- - - -

WILLIAM IV COPPER 34mm

Date	Mintage	Fine	V.F.	E.F.	abt. Unc/FDC
1831	806,400 P1455	£4	£24	£70	£140/£250
1831	Bronzed proofs	- - -	- - -	£90	£135/£200
1831	.W.W incuse initials	- - -	£30	£120	£300
1831	W.W. incuse initials	- - -	£34	£150	£325
1834	322,560	£6	£24	£90	£175/£300
1837	174,720	£8	£40	£130	£245/£365

PENNIES COPPER abt.

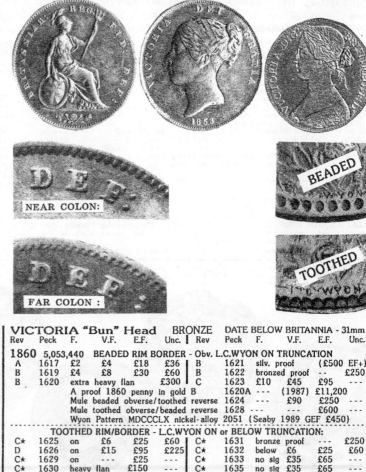

VICTORIA Young Head — DATE BELOW HEAD 34mm

Date	Mintage		Peck	Fine	V.F.	E.F.	Unc/FDC
1839	Bronzed proof		1479	DEF : o.t.	---	---	£185/£250
1841	913,920	REG	1480	£5	£17	£48	£150/£200
1841	Proofs			---	---	---	£250
1841	Proof in silver	(1980	As Struck)	---	---	£1,500
1841	No colon	REG	1484	£1	£5	£20	£40/£60
1843	483,830	REG:	1486	£15	£70	£220	£350/----
1843	No colon	REG	1485	£18	£75	£250	£450/----
1844	215,040		1487	£3	£7	£24	£60/£90
1845	322,560		1489	£4	£14	£50	£80/£130
1846	483,840	DEF :	1490	£3	£9	£40	£75/£110
1846		DEF:	1491	£4	£10	£46	£80/£125
1847	430,080	DEF :	1492	£2	£7	£30	£65/£100
1847		DEF :	1493	£2	£7	£30	£65/£100
1848	161,280		1496	£2	£7	£30	£60/£95
1848	8 over 6		1494	--	£22	£65	£120/£185
1848	8 over 7		1495	--	£5	£24	£75/£110
1849	268,800		1497	£25	£85	£250	£500/----
1851	432,224	DEF :	1498	£3	£7	£35	£90/£125
1851		DEF:	1499	£4	£12	£35	£120/£165
1853	1,021,440	DEF	1500	60p	£2	£20	£40/£60
1853	Narrow date			---	---	£12	£20/£40
1853	Proofs - copper and bronzed					---	£250
1853		DEF:	1503	£1	£6	£25	£75/£110
1853	Plain trident		1504	£2	£12	£30	£60/£90
1854	4 over 3		1505	£15	£45	£60	£100/£160
1854	6,720,000 p.t.		1506	£1	£4	£20	£40/£60
1854	Ornam trident		1507	---	£2	£9	£15/£35
1855	5,273,866 o.t.		1508	---	£4	£15	£25/£60
1855	Plain trident		1509	---	£3	£20	£40/£60
1856	1,212,288	DEF: p.t.	---	£9	£42	£90	£300/£375
1856	Plain trident proof		---	---	---		£250
1856		DEF : o.t.	---	£5	£35	£80	£250/£350
1857	752,640	DEF: p.t.	---	£1	£5	£15	£30/£50
1857		DEF : o.t.	---	£1	£5	£15	£30/£50
1857	Smaller date	p.t.	---	£1	£5	£15	£30/£50
1858	1,559,040:						
	8 over 3		1515	--	£22	£60	£90/---
	8 over 6			--	---	£60	
	8 over 7		1516	--	£3	£14	£35/---
	Smaller date		1517	£1	£4	£20	£45/£70
	Large date no W.W.		1518	65p	£3	£20	£40/£60
1859	1,075,200 Large date			£1	£6	£20	£60/£90
1859	9 over 8			£4	£16	£42	£95/£130
1859	Smaller date			£2	£8	£25	£80/----
1859	Proof			---	---	---	£950
1860	60 struck over 59			£100	£300	£600	£850/----

It is not unusual for the range Unc/FDC to vary thus:
Some lustre £12; Good lustre £20; Much lustre £28; Full lustre £35
DEF: = near colon - DEF : = far colon - o.t. = ornamental trident
plain tridents have near colons   p.t. = plain trident
All have ornamental tridents from 1839 to 1851

NEAR COLON: DEF.

FAR COLON : DEF.

BEADED

TOOTHED

VICTORIA "Bun" Head BRONZE DATE BELOW BRITANNIA - 31mm

Rev	Peck	F.	V.F.	E.F.	Unc.	Rev	Peck	F.	V.F.	E.F.	Unc.
1860	**5,053,440 BEADED RIM BORDER - Obv. L.C.WYON ON TRUNCATION**										
A	1617	£2	£4	£18	£36	B	1621	silv. proof		(£500 EF+)	
B	1619	£4	£8	£30	£60	B	1622	bronzed proof	--	£250	
B	1620	extra heavy flan		£300		C	1623	£10	£45	£95	---
	A proof 1860 penny in gold B						1620A	---	(1987)	£11,200	
	Mule beaded obverse/toothed reverse						1624	---	£90	£250	---
	Mule toothed obverse/beaded reverse						1628	---	---	£600	---
	Wyon Pattern MDCCCLX nickel-alloy 2051 (Seaby 1989 GEF £450)										
	TOOTHED RIM/BORDER - L.C.WYON ON or BELOW TRUNCATION:										
C★	1625	on	£6	£25	£60	C★	1631	bronze proof	---	£250	
D	1626	on	£15	£95	£225	C★	1632	below	£6	£25	£60
C★	1629	on	---	£25	---	C★	1633	no sig	£35	£65	
C★	1630	heavy flan		£150	---	C★	1635	no sig	£35	£65	
	ONF PENNY variety: damaged die 1634 £35 fair (1988) ---										

VICTORIA "Bun Head" DATE BELOW BRITANNIA - 31mm

Rev	Peck	F.	V.F.	E.F.	Unc.	Rev	Peck	F.	V.F.	E.F.	Unc.

1861 36,449,280 : L.C.WYON ON or BELOW TRUNCATION

Rev	Peck		F.	V.F.	E.F.	Unc.	Rev	Peck		F.	V.F.	E.F.	Unc.
C*	1637	on	£90	---	---		C*	1643	no sig	£25	---	---	
F	1638	no sig	£50	---	---		C*	1644	no sig	---	£20	---	
C*	1639	below	---	£18	---			6 over 8	£50	fair (1988)			
F	1642	no sig	£20	fair (1988)			F	1646	no sig	£5	£15		

OBVERSE 5 - NO SIGNATURE - WREATH OF 16 LEAVES - RAISED MIDRIBS
REVERSE F - NO SIGNATURE - THUMB DOES NOT TOUCH ST.GEORGE'S CROSS

Date	Mintage	F.	V.F.	E.F.	Unc.	Date	Mintage	F.	V.F.	E.F.	Unc.
1862	50,534,400	£1	£4	£16	£40	1865	5 over 3	£15	£45	£200	£425
1862	Bronzed proof --- --- ---				£250	1865	Pattern bronze P2061			nrFDC	£300
1862	Date from halfpenny die (smaller):					1866	9,999,360	£1	£6	£22	£55
	£60 fair (1988)					1867	5,483,520	£2	£9	£25	£75
1862	8 over 6	(Seaby 1989 GVF £275)				1868	1,182,720	£3	£18	£55	£125
1862	Pattern cu-nickel P2060	(FDC £600)				1868	Bronze proof P1681			---	£250
1863	28,062,720	£1	£4	£20	£50	1868	Copper-nickel proof			£200	£365
1863	Bronzed proof --- --- ---				£250	1869	2,580,480	£15	£65	£250	£525
1863	Die number below date:					1870	5,695,022	(Spink 1988 UNC £165)			
	3 below 1860 (fair 1988)					1870		(Seaby 1989 EF £60)			
1864	3,440,646 Plain 4	£28	£125	£325		1871	1,290,318	£6	£45	£100	£225
1864	Crosslet 4	£45	£200	£425		1872	8,494,572	£1	£8	£30	£75
1865	8,601,600	£2	£9	£45	£90	1873	8,494,200	£1	£8	£30	£75

OBVERSE 5; and OBVERSE 6 (a MORE MATRONLY PORTRAIT)
REVERSE F; and REVERSE G (a LESS GRACEFUL BRITANNIA)

O/R	Peck	F.	V.F.	E.F.	Unc.	O/R	Peck	F.	V.F.	E.F.	Unc.
1874 5,621,86 :						**1874H 6,666,240 :**					
5/F	1690	£2	£10	£40	£75	5/F	1694	£1	£4	£20	£45
5/G	1691	£2	£10	£40	£75	5/G	1695	£2	£12	£45	£80
5/G	1692	£1	£8	£30	£65	6/F	1696	£1	£4	£20	£45
6/G	1693	£1	£8	£25	£60	6/F	1697	£1	£4	£18	£40
						6/G	1698	Bronze proof		---	£250

1860 reverse: L.C.W. incuse below shield
Rev. A = crosses outlined with treble incuse lines, no rock
Rev. B = crosses outlined by close, double, raised lines, no rock
Rev. C = similar to Rev. B, but small rock to left of lighthouse
Rev. C* = as Rev. C, but with minor modifications to rocks and sea
Rev. D = as Rev. C, but L.C.W. incuse below foot
Rev. E = no signature, thumb touches St.George's Cross; no vertical lines to lantern
Rev. F = no signature, thumb does not touch Cross, lantern has six vertical lines
Rev. G = Britannia has long, thin neck; her helmet is tall and narrow; a tall, thin lighthouse

Date	Mintage	F.	V.F.	E.F.	Unc.	Date	Mintage	F.	V.F.	E.F.	Unc.
1875	10,691,040	£1	£5	£16	£40	1882H	7,526,400	£1	£5	£16	£30
1875H	752,640	£8	£45	£150	£300	1883	6,237,438	£1	£6	£20	£45
1875H	Proof P1706	---	nFDC		£350	1884	11,702,802	£1	£3	£12	£30
1876H	11,074,560	£1	£5	£16	£30	1885	7,145,862	£1	£3	£12	£30
1877	9,624,747	£1	£5	£20	£35	1886	6,087,759	60p	£3	£14	£26
1877	Proof cupro-nickel		nFDC		£700	1887	5,315,085	60p	£3	£14	£26
1878	2,764,470	£2	£9	£30	£50	1887	Aluminium pattern (P2175)				£375
1878	Proof P1713	---	nFDC		£275	1888	5,125,020	60p	£3	£12	£25
1879	7,666,476	£1	£5	£16	£30	1889	12,559,737	50p	£3	£12	£25
1879	Re-touched Obv. P1715		£30	GEF			Narrow date (P1745)		£25	---	
1880	3,000,831	£2	£9	£40	£50	1890	15,330,840	50p	£3	£12	£25
1881	2,302,261	£2	£10	£42	£65	1891	17,885,961	30p	£2	£10	£16
1881	Portrait 'aged' further:					1892	10,501,671	30p	£2	£12	£20
	P1722	£2	£12	£50	£75	1893	8,161,737	40p	£3	£12	£22
1881H	3,763,200	£1	£5	£16	£30	1894	3,883,452	£2	£5	£15	£34
1881H	Heraldically coloured shield				£45	Proofs for 1881, 1884/85/86 and 1890/91/92					

VICTORIA - Old, Veiled, or Widow Head

Date	Mintage	F.	V.F.	E.F.	Unc.	Date	Mintage	F.	V.F.	E.F.	Unc.
1895	5,395,830 Rev B	£1	£5	£10		1897	Higher horizon (Spink'88)				£100
1895	No sea Rev A	£2	£15	£75	£165	1898	14,296,836	15p	£1	£4	£12
1895	Pattern (P2066)		nFDC		£720	1899	26,441,069	15p	£1	£4	£8
1896	24,147,156	15p	£1	£4	£8	1900	31,778,109	---	50p	£3	£6
1896	9 and 6 further apart	£1	£5	£9		1901	22,205,568	---	50p	£2	£4
1897	20,756,620	15p	£1	£4	£8						

1895 Rev A, trident to P is 2mm; no sea behind
1895 Rev B, trident to P is 1mm; sea behind (to left of) Britannia
1895 Pattern, only five known, (1985 FDC) £1200
Full lustre and/or abt.FDC can add 50% to Unc. value

Date	Mintage	Fine	V.F.	E.F.	abt. Unc/FDC
EDWARD VII				BRONZE 31 mm	
1902	26,976,768	30p	£2	£4	£8/£12
1902	LOW TIDE variety	£1	£4	£15	£30/£45
1903	21,415,296	---	---	£8	£12/£21
1903	Open '3' Fair £30 (Spink 1988)			---	---/---
1904	12,913,152	---	---	£12	£18/£30
1905	17,783,808	---	£1.50	£10	£16/£25
1906	37,989,504	---	£3	£6	£12/£18
1907	47,322,240	---	£2	£9	£12/£18
1908	31,506,048	---	£2	£10	£15/£25
1909	19,617,024	---	£1	£6	£14/£20
1909	Noted 1994 (Cooke)		"BU Full Lustre 'blazing'"		£32
1910	29,549,184	---	£1	£5	£10/£15
GEORGE V				BRONZE 31 mm	
1911	23,079,168	(1 + A)	£2	£5	£8/£12
1911	Hollow neck	(see page 6)	(1988 GEF £20)		---
1912	48,306,048	(1 + A)	£1	£5	£10/£24
1912H	16,800,000	(1 + A)	£3	£15	£20/£30
1913	65,497,872	(2 + B)	£2	£5	£10/£20
1914	50,820,997	---	£2	£4	£10/£15
1915	47,310,807	---	£2	£5	£10/£15
1916	86,411,165	---	£1	£3	£9/£12
1917	107,905,436	---	£1	£3	£9/£12
1918	84,227,372	---	£1	£3	£6/£9
1918H	3,660,800	£1	£6	£65	£120/---
1918KN	Inc above	£2	£8	£75	£150/---
1919	113,761,090	---	£1	£3	£10/£15
1919H	5,209,600	£1	£5	£90	£110/£175
1919KN	Inc above	£2	£10	£90	£180/£225
1920	124,693,485	(2 + B)	£1	£3	£6/£10
1920	(P2259)	(3 + B)	---	---	---/---
1921	129,717,693	(2 + B)	£1	£3	£6/£12
1921	(P2261)	(3 + B)	£1	£3	£6/£12
1922	16,346,711	(3 + B)	£1.50	£10	£15/£30
1923 to 1925	None	---	---	---	---
1926	4,498,519	---	£3	£16	£20/£40
1926	Modified effigy	£3	£20	£200	£450/£650
1927	60,989,561	---	£1	£2	£4/£6
1928	50,178,000 smaller head	---	£1	£2	£3/£6
1929	49,132,800	---	50p	£2	£3/£6
1930	29,097,600	---	60p	£4	£6/£9
1931	19,843,200	---	75p	£5	£10/£15
1932	8,277,600	---	£2	£15	£24/£40
1932	Proof (P2278)	---		nFDC	£150
1933	8 plus "patterns"			(1986)	£18,975
1933	Pattern by Lavrillier			(1986)	£4,100
1933	A uniface		(1980 £28,750)		£50,000
1934	13,965,600	---	£1	£5	£12/£22
1935	56,070,000	---	50p	£1	£2/£4
1935	Bronze proof Noted 1994	---		FDC	£220
1936	154,296,000	---	---	£1	£2/£4

Proofs for all dates from 1926 to 1936 except 1933

Vertical annotations in Fine/V.F. columns:
Obv 1, bottom stop of colon close to A, GRA:BRITT
Obv 2, stops are midway but cramped, GRA:BRITT
Obv 3, as Obv 2, but words GRA: BRITT: farther apart.
Toothed circle of rev A has 163 teeth whilst B has 188

KN-Kings Norton Mint Mark

H.-Heaton Mint Mark

In addition to the eight pennies listed at left (left-hand pair above); there were patterns, possibly four, struck from dies engraved by André Lavrillier (right-hand pair above) having a 'military' King George V, a thick trident and a sea of wavy lines. Yet another 1933 penny is uniface: having a "tail" but the "head" replaced by the word MODEL. The 1933 set from St. Mary's Church, Hawksworth Wood, was offered for sale at Sotheby's in 1972. It fetched £7,000. This set was one of those placed under foundation stones laid by King George in 1933.

Date	Mintage	Fine	V.F.	E.F.	abt. Unc/FDC
EDWARD VIII (Duke of Windsor)					Bronze 31 mm
1937	Specimen strikings only				
GEORGE VI					Bronze 31 mm
1937	88,896,000	---	10p	50p	£1/£2
1937	26,402 proofs	---	---		/£5
1938	121,560,000	---	10p	65p	£1/£2
1939	55,560,000	---	30p	£1	£3/£5
1940	42,284,400	---	50p	£2	£5/£7
1941 to 1943 none		---	---	---	---
1944	42,600,000	---	30p	£2	£4/£6
1945	79,531,200	---	25p	£1.50	£3/£5
1945	Doubled 9	£1	£5	£25	---
1946	66,855,600	---	15p	£1	£2/£3
1947	52,220,400	---	15p	£1	£2/£3
1948	63,961,200	---	5p	25p	50p/£2
1949	14,324,400	---	10p	60p	£1/£2
1950	240,000	£2	£4	£6	£12/£18
1950	17,513 proofs	---	---	---	/£15
1951	120,000	£3	£6	£9	£18/£25
1951	20,000 proofs	---	---	---	£12/£15
	Proofs for all dates except, possibly, 1947 ••••				
1937	Rev Aa	Ns point to border teeth		N N	
1937	Rev Ab	Ns point between teeth (b is rarer)		N N	••••
1940	Rev Ab	has single exergue line			
1940	Rev B	has double exergue line (Ab is rarer)			
1944	Rev Ba	waves touch exergue			
1944	Rev Bb	gap between waves and exergue			

(POINTINGS - page 33)

Date	Mintage	Fine	V.F.	E.F.	abt. Unc/FDC
ELIZABETH II					Bronze 31 mm
1953	Pattern (not in Peck) unique ? : has toothed (not beaded) border Spink £1,950				
1953	1,308,400 (the 'Plastic' Set)	---		£1	£2/£4
1953	40,000 proofs	---	---		£5/£6
1953	Pattern from sand-blasted dies	---		£300	(1985)
1954	1 retrieved from change. Now in British Museum.				
1954	(Another, or the same one?) Purchased in 1992 for £21,000				
1955 to 1960 none		---	---	---	---
1961	48,313,400	---	---	---	25p/60p
1962	157,588,600	---	---	---	20p/50p
1963	119,733,600	---	---	---	---/15p
1964	153,294,000	---	---	---	12p/25p
1965	121,310,400	---	---	---	10p/20p
1965	In gold, unofficial, (Christies 1989)	---			£1300
1966	165,739,200	---	---	---	---/10p
1966	2 (so far) Jersey penny obverse. Auction 1992				£605
1967	155,280,000	---	---	---	---/10p
1968	170,400,000 all dated 1967				
1969	219,360,000 all dated 1967				
1970	109,524,000 all dated 1967:	654,564,000			
	Proofs for some dates. 1970 proofs, from sets, £1/£2				

THREE HALFPENCES   ISSUED FOR COLONIAL USE

Date	Mintage	Fine	V.F.	E.F.	abt. Unc/FDC
WILLIAM IV		Silver 12 mm			
1834	800,448	45p	£2	£8	£16/£25
1835	633,600	70p	£3	£12	£24/£36
1835	5 struck over 4	£2	£10	£40	£80/---
1836	158,400	70p	£3	£12	£24/£36
1837	30,624	£4	£16	£65	£120/£180
VICTORIA		Silver 12 mm			
1838	538,560	60p	£3	£12	£25/£40
1839	760,320	35p	£2	£8	£18/£25
1840	95,040	£1	£5	£20	£36/£60
1841	158,400	50p	£2	£8	£16/£30
1842	1,869,120	50p	£2	£8	£16/£30
1843	475,200	30p	£2	£8	£16/£30
1843	43 over 34	£2	£8	£30	£60/---
1860	160,000	£1	£4	£16	£36/£50
1862	256,000	£1	£3	£16	£25/£40
1862	Proof	(Seaby 1990) abt.FDC			£475
1870	Proof, or pattern	(1986) ---		---	£325

TWO PENCES
For COPPER TWOPENCES see page 11

Date	Mintage	Fine	V.F.	E.F.	abt. Unc/FDC

GEORGE III   SILVER · 18 mm until 1817

Date	Mintage	Fine	V.F.	E.F.	abt. Unc/FDC
1762		£2	£5	£10	£20/£30
1763		£2	£5	£10	£20/£30
1763	proof	- - -	- - -	- - -	- - -
1765	extremely rare	£100	£250	£600	- - -/- - -
1765	Noted (1991)	(Seaby, nearly E.F. £550)			- - -/- - -
1766		£3	£8	£16	£32/£48
1770		£3	£8	£18	£36/£50
1772	large lettering	£3	£8	£16	£32/£48
1772	small lettering	£3	£8	£16	£32/£48
1780		£2	£6	£12	£25/£40
1784		£3	£8	£16	£32/£48
1786		£3	£8	£16	£32/£48
1792	WIRE MONEY	£7	£16	£32	£50/£85
1795	normal figure 3	£3	£7	£15	£28/- - -
1800		£3	£7	£15	£28/- - -

NOW reduced to 17 mm:

Date	Mintage	Fine	V.F.	E.F.	abt. Unc/FDC
1817	BULL HEAD	30p	£3	£14	£24/£36
1818		30p	£3	£15	£25/- - -
1820		50p	£3	£14	£22/£36

GEORGE IV   SILVER · 17 mm

Date	Mintage	Fine	V.F.	E.F.	abt. Unc/FDC
1822	small head	£1	£3	£18	£30/£36
1822	from Maundy proof set	- - -	- - -		
1823	larger normal head	50p	£2	£10	£18/£25
1824		50p	£3	£12	£20/£32
1825		50p	£2	£10	£18/£25
1826		50p	£2	£10	£18/£25
1827		50p	£2	£10	£18/£25
1828		50p	£2	£10	£18/£25
1828	from Maundy proof set	- - -	- - -		- - -/- - -
1829		50p	£2	£10	£18/£25
1830		50p	£2	£10	£18/£25

WILLIAM IV   Silver 17 mm

Date	Mintage	Fine	V.F.	E.F.	abt. Unc/FDC
1831	from Maundy set	50p	£4	£20	£30/£50
1831	from Maundy proof set	- - -	- - -		£36
1832	from Maundy set	50p	£4	£16	£21/£36
1833	from Maundy set	50p	£4	£16	£21/£36

For use in West Indies - unpolished surface:

Date	Mintage	Fine	V.F.	E.F.	abt. Unc/FDC
1834	401,016	£1	£5	£20	£40/£60
1835	491,040	£1	£5	£20	£40/£60
1836	411,840	£1	£4	£18	£36/£55
1837	42,768	£2	£7	£25	£50/£75

VICTORIA   Young Head   as Maundy but 'dull' surface

Date	Mintage	Fine	V.F.	E.F.	abt. Unc/FDC
1838	1,203,840	75p	£4	£20	£40/£60
1838	reads BRITANNIAB (error)	- - -	- - -		
1839	570,240	£2	£5	£30	£60/£90
1840	633,600	£2	£6	£35	£70/£95
1841	443,520	£2	£5	£40	£80/- - -
1842	2,027,520	£2	£5	£40	£80/- - -
1843	included above	£1	£3	£20	£40/£65
1844	1,045,400	£1	£5	£35	£70/£95
Preceding coins were for use only in the colonies.					
1845	1,314,720	£1	£4	£14	£20/£40
1845	Noted (D.J.Traynor 1990)		BU Gem		£25
1846	47,520	£3	£6	£50	£95/- - -
1849	126,720	£1	£5	£35	£70/£95
1850	950,400	£1	£3	£15	£30/£50
1851	479,065	£1	£3	£25	£50/£75
1853	31,680	£1	£5	£50	£100/- - -
1854	1,467,246	£1	£5	£25	£50/£75
1855	383,350	£1	£5	£40	£80/- - -
1856	1,013,760	£1	£5	£35	£70/- - -
1857	1,758,240	£1	£5	£35	£70/- - -
1858	1,441,440	£1	£5	£35	£70/£95
1858	BRITANNIAB (error)	- -	- - -		- - -/- - -
1859	3,579,840	£1	£3	£10	£20/£35
1860	3,405,600	£1	£4	£20	£40/£60
1861	3,294,720	£1	£3	£15	£30/£45
1862	1,156,320	£1	£4	£25	£45/£65
1863	950,400	£1	£5	£35	£65/- - -
1864	1,330,560	£1	£3	£20	£40/£60
1865	1,742,400	£1	£5	£35	£70/£95
1866	1,900,800	£1	£3	£20	£40/£60
1867	712,800	£1	£4	£25	£50/£75
1868	1,457,280	£1	£3	£20	£40/£60
1868	RRITANNIAR error	£12	£40	£150	- - -/- - -
1868	Laureate Head pattern by Wyon		- - -		- - -/- - -
1869	Colonial only Noted 1993		- - -		£250

THREEPENCES

SILVER 16.5 mm

Date	Mintage	Fine	V.F.	E.F.	abt. Unc/FDC
VICTORIA YOUNG HEAD					
1870	1,283,218	£1	£3	£15	£30/£45
1871	999,633	£1	£3	£20	£40/£50
1872	1,293,271	£1	£3	£15	£30/£45
1873	4,055,550	£1	£2.50	£11	£25/---
1874	4,427,031	£1	£2.50	£11	£25/---
1875	3,306,500	£1	£2.50	£11	£25/---
1876	1,834,389	£1	£2.50	£11	£25/---
1877	2,622,393	£1	£2.50	£11	£20/£30
1878	2,419,975	£1	£2.50	£11	£20/£30
1879	3,140,265	£1	£2.50	£11	£20/£30
1880	1,610,069	£1	£3	£15	£25/£40
1881	3,248,265	£1	£3	£15	£22/£40
1882	472,965	£2	£4	£25	£45/£70
1883	4,365,971	£1	£2	£7	£14/£20
1884	3,322,424	£1	£2	£7	£14/£20
1885	5,183,653	£1	£2	£7	£14/£20
1886	6,152,669	£1	£2	£7	£14/£20
1887	2,780,761 Yg Hd	£1	£3	£15	£30/£45
	Young Head proof	---	---	---	---
JUBILEE HEAD					
1887	Included above	50p	£1	£3	£5/£8
1887	Jubilee Head proof	---	---	---	£35/£45
1888	518,199	£1	£2	£8	£15/£25
1889	4,587,010	£1	£2	£6	£12/£20
1890	4,465,834	£1	£2	£6	£12/£20
1891	6,323,027	£1	£2	£4	£8/£12
1892	2,578,226	£1	£2	£6	£12/£20
1893	3,067,243 Jub Hd	£5	£10	£25	£50/£90
OLD or WIDOW HEAD					
1893	Included above	60p	£1	£2	£6/£9
1893	1,312 Proofs	---	---	---	£35/£50
1894	1,608,603	60p	£1	£4	£9/£15
1895	4,788,609	60p	£1	£4	£9/£15
1896	4,598,442	60p	£1	£4	£9/£15
1897	4,541,294	60p	£1	£3	£6/£9
1898	4,567,177	60p	£1	£3	£6/£9
1899	6,246,281	60p	£1	£3	£6/£9
1900	10,644,480	75p	£2	£3	£6/£10
1901	6,098,400	50p	£1	£3	£6/£9

★ Threepences bearing dates not listed are, probably, Maundy pieces.

SILVER 16.5 mm

Date	Mintage	Fine	V.F.	E.F.	abt. Unc/FDC
EDWARD VII					
1902	8,268,480	65p	£1	£3	£5/£8
1902	15,123 proofs	---	---	---	£10/£15
1903	5,227,200	£1	£2	£6	£12/£18
1904	3,627,360	£2	£4	£20	£40/£50
1905	3,548,160	£1	£2	£15	£30/£40
1906	3,152,160	£1	£4	£12	£24/£36
1907	4,831,200	80p	£2	£6	£12/£20
1908	8,157,600	£1	£2	£6	£12/£20
1909	4,055,040	£1	£2	£6	£12/£20
1910	4,563,380	75p	£2	£8	£10/£18
GEORGE V	SILVER (.925 to 1920 then .500) 16.5mm				
1911	5,841,084	75p	£2	£3	£6/£10
1911	6,001 proofs	---	---	---	£20
1912	8,932,825	60p	£1	£2	£5/£8
1913	7,143,242	60p	£1	£2	£5/£8
1914	6,733,584	60p	£1	£2	£5/£8
1915	5,450,617	60p	£2	£4	£5/£8
1916	18,555,201	60p	£1	£3	£5/£8
1917	21,662,490	60p	£1	£2	£3/£5
1918	20,630,909	60p	£1	£2	£3/£5
1919	16,845,687	60p	£1	£2	£3/£5
1920	16,703,597	50p	75p	£2	£4/£6
1920	.500 silver	50p	75p	£2	£4/£6
1921	8,749,301	50p	75p	£2	£3/£5
1922	7,979,998	50p	£1	£2	£3/£5
1923	Small number of patterns, struck in nickel			--	--
1925	3,731,859	£1	£2	£6	£12/£18
1925	Patterns, in nickel, of new (1927) design			--	--
1926	4,107,910	£1	£3	£12	£22/£36
1926	Modified Effigy	50p	£1.50	£6	£12/£18

> 1904 Large '3' closer to bow at bottom and crown at top.
> 1911 Obv. 1a = neck hollow } as described on page 6.
>   Obv. 1b = neck flat

SILVER THREEPENCES

Date	Mintage		Fine	V.F.	E.F.	abt. Unc/FDC

GEORGE V — SILVER (50%) 16.5mm

Date	Mintage		Fine	V.F.	E.F.	abt. Unc/FDC
1927	15,022 proofs oak sprig/acorn reverse				--	£25/£35
1928	1,302,106		75p	£2	£5	£10/£15
1929	None		---	---	---	---/---
1930	1,319,412		40p	£1	£4	£8/£12
1931	6,251,936		25p	50p	£1	£2/£4
1932	5,887,325		25p	50p	£1	£2/£4
1933	5,578,541		25p	50p	£1	£2/£4
1934	7,405,954		25p	50p	£2	£4/£6
1934	A proof offered for sale in 1976 (!)					/£55
1935	7,027,654		12p	25p	£1	£2/£3
1936	3,238,670		10p	20p	£1	£2/£3

EDWARD VIII (Duke of Windsor)
A PATTERN BEARING A DESIGN OF THREE RINGS

GEORGE VI — SILVER (50%) 16.5mm

Date	Mintage		Fine	V.F.	E.F.	abt. Unc/FDC
1937	8,148,156		25p	50p	70p	£1.50/£2
1937	26,402 proofs		---	---	---	£3/£5
1938	6,402,473		---	25p	50p	£1/£2
1939	1,355,860		25p	50p	£1	£3/£5
1940	7,914,401		20p	45p	60p	£1.50/£2
1941	7,979,411		25p	50p	£1	£2/£3
1942	4,144,051 Colonial		£1	£2	£5	£9/£15
1943	1,379,220 Colonial		£1	£3	£6	£10/£16
1944	2,005,553 Colonial		£2	£6	£10	£15/£20
1945	371,000 dated 1944; re-melted by The Mint					
	One dated 1945 is known to have 'escaped'.					

NICKEL-BRASS THREEPENCES

Date	Mintage	Fine	V.F.	E.F.	Unc/abt FDC

EDWARD VIII Duke of Windsor — DODECAGONAL

Date		
1937	Date divided by THRIFT PLANT (Sea-pink); a few were made for slot machine testing and thicknesses vary.	Spinks (1990) £28.500 Cooke (1994) £24.500
1937	Date at bottom, but effigy Edward VIII. Certainly rarer than that listed above. Lettering is EDWARDVS VIII *not* GEORGVS VI.	

GEORGE VI — DODECAGONAL - MODIFIED THRIFT PLANT

Date	Mintage		Fine	V.F.	E.F.	Unc/abt FDC
1937	45,707,957		---	15p	50p	£1/£2
1937	26,402 proofs		---	---		£4
1938	14,532,332		5p	30p	£3	£5/£8
1939	5,603,021		12p	60p	£4	£15/£20
1940	12,636,018		10p	50p	£2	£4/£6
1941	60,239,489		---	15p	£1	£2/£3
1942	103,214,400		---	12p	£1	£2/£3
1943	101,702,400		---	12p	50p	£1/£2
1944	69,760,000		---	15p	50p	£1/£3
1945	33,942,466		---	20p	£1.25	£3/£6
1946	620,734		£1	£5	£30	£125/£155
1946	Noted 1994		---	"gd E.F."	£67	----/----
1946	Proof		(1985)	---	---	FDC £250
1947	None		---	---	---	---
1948	4,230,400		12p	£1	£3	£6/£10
	IND. IMP discontinued					
1949	464,000		£1	£5	£30	£60/£90
1949	A proof in brass		---	---	---	£200
1950 }*	1,600,000		10p	£1	£8	£20/£40
1950 }	17,513 proofs		---	---	---	£10/£15
1951	1,184,000		10p	£1	£8	£20/£40
1951	20,000 proofs		---	---	---	£20
1952	25,494,400		---	20p	70p	£1/£2
	British Museum has proof/s of each date					

1937   Two different spacings from rim of word THREE noted :
     Rev. A = large gap;   Rev. B = small gap

* A "Strange Madness" when a superb proof striking costs less than one struck for general circulation.

Sharp v Rounded Corners:	
1937 - 1940	All sharp
1941	Both
1942 - 1946	All rounded
1948	Both
1949	All rounded
1950 - 1952	All sharp

   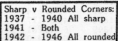

NICKEL - BRASS THREEPENCES
DODECAGONAL

Date	Mintage		Fine	V.F.	E.F.	abt. Unc/ FDC

ELIZABETH II   PORTCULLIS with CHAINS, ROYALLY CROWNED

Date	Mintage		Fine	V.F.	E.F.	abt. Unc/FDC
1953	30,618,000	BRITT.OMN	25p	50p	75p/£1.50
1953	40,000	proofs Obv.2	---	---	£2/£4
1954	41,720,000	no BRITT.OMN	25p	50p	£2/£4
1954	Matt proof	(1982 - Seaby)			£90
1955	41,075,200	---	25p	50p	£1/£2
1956	36,801,600	---	45p	£1	£2/£4
1957	24,294,400	---	25p	£1.50	£3/£6
1958	20,504,000	---	45p	£1	£4/£8
1958	Proof	(Coincraft 1993)		FDC	£275
1959	28,499,200	---	---	50p	£2/£3
1960	83,078,400	---	---	25p	£1/£2
1961	41,102,400	---	---	20p	40p/95p
1962	51,545,600	---	---	20p	40p/95p
1963	35,280,000	---	---	20p	40p/95p
1964	44,867,200	---	---	5p	10p/40p
1965	27,160,000	---	---	5p	10p/40p
1966	53,760,000	---	---	---	10p/40p
1967	151,780,800	---	---	---	5p/20p
1970	750,476	proofs for LAST STERLING set		F.D.C.	£2

V.A.T., not included here, is sometimes
absorbed by the seller on a 'special offer' basis.

1953	(a) = I of ELIZABETH points to corner of rim/edge.
	(b) = I is much further to the right (see page 33).
1953	Obv. 1 Details, particularly head ribbon and initials M.G. are poorly defined = ex-specimen set (page 48).
	Obv. 2 Portrait more sharply outlined as are the ends of the head ribbon = normal issue.
	Both have ovoid stops.
1954	Much sharper overall and with round stops.

FOURPENCES or GROATS

GEORGE III   Reverse has LARGE FIGURE 4 · SILVER 19.5mm

Date	Mintage		Fine	V.F.	E.F.	abt. Unc/FDC
1763		Young Armoured Bust	£2	£7	£16	---/---
1763		Extremely rare proof	---	---	---	---/---
1765		Extremely rare currency	£100	£200	£500	---/---
1766			£4	£8	£16	---/---
1770			£4	£8	£16	---/---
1772			£4	£8	£16	---/---
1772		2 struck over 0	£4	£16	£32	---/---
1776			£3	£6	£12	---/---
1780			£3	£6	£12	---/---
1784			£4	£8	£16	---/---
1786			£4	£8	£16	---/---
1792		Thin 4 (wire money)	£6	£12	£24	---/---
1794		Normal 4 from Maundy	£3	£8	£16	---/---
1800		Also from Maundy	£3	£6	£12	---/---

WILLIAM IV   Reverse has FOUR PENCE in words - SILVER 16.5mm

Date	Mintage		Fine	V.F.	E.F.	abt. Unc/FDC
1836		Britannia seated : D :	£1	£2	£12	£20/£30
1836		Colons close to :D:	---	£6	£18	---/---
1836		Proofs, grained (milled) edge in silver		---	---/---
1836		Proofs, plain edge in gold - -		---	---/---
1836		Proofs, plain edge in silver	£275	£350	---/---
1837	962,280		£1	£2	£10	£20/£30

A number of patterns exist

The FOURPENCE, not the silver threepence, is the true "Joey": taking its
name from one Joseph Hume who recommended it to facilitate payment
of the, then, 4d London omnibus fare.

FOURPENCES or GROATS

Date	Mintage	Fine	V.F.	E.F.	abt. Unc/FDC
VICTORIA	FOUR PENCE in words - SILVER 16.5mm				
1837	Proof only - plain edged		---		---
1837	Proof only - grained (milled) edge			---	
1838	2,150,280	£1	£3	£12	£28/£40
1838	2nd 8 struck over ∞	£1	£3	£20	£45/£65
1838	Plain edged proof	---	---	---	£120
1839	1,461,240	£1	£3	£12	£24/£35
1839	Plain edged proof from the sets			---	£130
1840	1,496,880	£1	£3	£10	£20/£30
1841	344,520	£2	£7	£25	£48/£75
1842	724,680	£1	£3	£12	£36/£50
1842	Plain edged proof	---	---	---	£130
1842	2 struck over 1	£3	£8	£50	---
1843	1,817,640	£1	£3	£18	£36/£54
1844	855,360	£1	£4	£20	£48/£68
1845	914,760	£1	£4	£20	£45/£65
1846	1,366,200	60p	£3	£16	£32/£50
1847	7 struck over 6	£15	£32	£95	£120/£175
1848	712,800	£3	£6	£16	£36/---
1848	2nd 8 over 6	£2	£5	£20	£45/£65
1848	2nd 8 over 7	£2	£5	£20	£45/£65
1849	380,160	£1	£4	£19	£40/---
1849	9 struck over 8	£2	£7	£30	£60/£80
1851	594,000	£12	£50	£140	£180/£250
1852	31,300	£25	£80	£200	£350/----
1853	11,880	£30	£90	£250	£450/----
1853	Grained (milled) edge proof from set			---	£300
1853	Plain edged proof	---	---	£150	----
1854	1,096,613	£1	£3	£15	£25/£36
1854	5 struck over 3	£1	£3	£18	£36/---
1855	646,041	£1	£3	£16	£32/---
1857	Proof only, grained edge		---	---	£650
1862	Proof only, plain edge		---	---	£450
1888	JUBILEE HEAD (Br.Guiana)	£8	£20	£30/£50	
1888	Grained edge proof		---	---	

SIXPENCES

Date	Mintage/etc	Fine	V.F.	E.F.	Unc/abt FDC
GEORGE III	ARMOURED BUST to 1816 SILVER 21/22mm				
1786	Pattern - no hearts in Shield of Hanover				
1787	No hearts illustrations	£3	£7	£11	£16/£25
1787	With hearts page 29	£3	£7	£11	£16/£25
1787	Proof, without hearts	---	---		£275
1788	Pattern by Droz (ESC 1642)	---	£300		----
1790	Pattern by Droz (ESC 1645)	---	£250		----
1790	Pattern by Droz (ESC 1646)	---	£150		----
1791	Pattern by Droz (ESC 1647)	---	£300		----
	BULL HEAD		SILVER 19 mm		
1816	Included below	£1.50	£5	£12	£24/£36
1816	Proof in gold	---			---/---
1817	10,921,680 (inc 1816)	£3	£6	£15	£30/£45
1817	Proof, plain edge	---		(1985)	£300
1818	4,284,720	£3	£8	£25	£50/£80
1819	4,712,400	£2	£6	£20	£30/£50
1819	Very small 8	£4	£9	£36	£75/---
1820	1,448,960	£2	£6	£25	£36/£55
1820	Inverted 1 1820	£15	£45	£150	£240/---
GEORGE IV					SILVER 19mm
1820	Proof only, garnished shield		---		£600/£750
1821	863,280	£3	£14	£30	£60/£100
1821	Proof (ESC 1655) ---	---	---	---	£350/----
1821	BBITANNIAR error	£30	£60	£120	£240/£360
1824	633,600 gartered shield	£3	£14	£50	£110/£160
1825	483,120 gartered shield	£3	£14	£50	£110/£160
1825	Pattern for BARE HEAD design (Spink)			---	£2,000
1826	689,040	£8	£35	£125	£250/£325
1826	A proof - Shield within Garter ---				£125
	Type change to BARE HEAD - LION on CROWN reverse				
1826	Included above	£2	£8	£36	£50/£75
1826	A proof - Bare Head/Lion on Crown				£125/£200
1827	166,320	£6	£30	£80	£165/£220
1828	15,840 ?	£4	£24	£65	£125/----
1829	403,920	£3	£15	£60	£100/----
WILLIAM IV					SILVER 19mm
1831	1,340,195	£2	£10	£30	£65/£95
1831	A proof - plain edge	---	---	---	£75/£95
1834	5,892,480	£2	£10	£40	£90/£130
1835	1,552,320	£2	£10	£40	£90/£130
1836	1,987,920	£5	£20	£85	£120/---
1837	506,880	£3	£16	£60	£100/£150

VICTORIA — Young Head

SILVER 19mm

Date	Mintage/etc	Fine	V.F.	E.F.	abt. Unc/FDC
1838	1,607,760	£2	£8	£40	£75/£110
1839	3,310,560	£2	£7	£35	£70/£100
1839	A proof or pattern	---	---	---	£145/£160
1840	2,098,800	£3	£9	£38	£75/£110
1840	Pattern by W.Wyon rev cancelled with fine lines				---/---
1841	1,386,000	£3	£14	£45	£75/---
1841	Pattern, gold, using half-sovereign reverse				
1842	601,920	£3	£12	£45	£90/£130
1843	3,160,080	£2	£10	£40	£80/£120
1844	3,975,840	£2	£9	£32	£70/---
1844	Has large 44	£3	£12	£42	£90/---
1845	3,714,480	£2	£10	£40	£80/£120
1846	4,268,880	£2	£10	£35	£60/ £85
1847	Would seem to exist	---	---	---	---/---
1848	586,080	£12	£50	£130	£250/---
1848	8 struck over 6	---	£60	£145	£250/---
1848	8 struck over 7	---	£60	£145	£250/---
1850	498,960	£3	£10	£45	£100/---
1850	5 struck over 3	---	(Cooke 1990 abt.BU £99)		
1851	2,288,107	£2	£9	£36	£75/£120
1852	904,586	£2	£9	£36	£75/£120
1853	3,837,930	£2	£8	£25	£40/ £70
1853	A proof	---	---	---	£300
1854	840,116	£25	£85	£300	----
1855	1,129,084	£2	£9	£32	£65/ £95
1855	A proof	---	---	---	£250
1856	2,779,920	£2	£9	£32	£65/ £95
1856	A pattern worded	HALF	SHILLING		----
1856	A pattern worded	1/2	SHILLING		----
1857	2,233,440	£2	£9	£32	£65/ £95
1858	1,932,480	£2	£9	£32	£65/ £95
1858	A Proof	---	---	---	£250
1859	4,688,640	£2	£9	£30	£60/ £90
1859	9 struck over 8	(Spink 1988 GEF £145)			---/---
1860	1,100,880	£2	£9	£35	£75/£120
1862	990,000	£10	£35	£115	£250/---
1863	491,040	£6	£25	£85	£150/---

NOW WITH DIE NUMBER (above date, below wreath)

Date	Mintage/etc	Fine	V.F.	E.F.	abt. Unc/FDC
1864	4,253,040	£2	£9	£40	£65/ £95
1865	1,631,520	£2	£12	£45	£75/---
1866	5,140,080	£2	£9	£40	£70/£105
1866	No die number	£18	£65	£200	---
1867	1,362,240	£3	£16	£50	£95/---
1867	A proof	---	---	---	£250
1868	1,069,200	£3	£16	£50	£95/---
1869	388,080	£3	£17	£52	£95/£145
1869	A proof	---	---	---	£180/----

1856 Variety: longer line below PENCE - rare
1857 Variety: longer line below PENCE - rare

VICTORIA (continued)

DIE NUMBER above date, below wreath

Date	Mintage	Fine	V.F.	E.F.	Unc/abt FDC
1870	479,613	£4	£15	£60	£90/£145
1870	A proof	---	---	---	£155
1871	3,662,684	£2	£8	£25	£50/ £80
1871	A proof	---	---	---	£160
1871	No die number	£3	£12	£50	£75/ ---
1871	A proof without die number	---	---	---	£225
1872	3,382,048 die no.	£2	£8	£20	£40/ £60
1873	4,594,733 die no.	£2	£8	£20	£40/ £60
1874	4,225,726 die no.	£2	£8	£20	£40/ £60
1875	3,256,545 die no.	£2	£8	£20	£40/ £60
1876	841,435 die no.	£4	£12	£50	£75/£112
1877	4,066,486 die no.	£2	£8	£20	£40/ ---
1877	No die number	£2	£8	£25	£45/ ---
1878	2,624,525 die no.	£2	£8	£20	£40/ ---
1878	A proof of previous coin	---	---	---	£155
1878	8 struck over 7	---	---	---	----
1878	DRITANNIAR error	£15	£45	£200	---
1879	3,326,313	£4	£12	£40	£65/£100

DIE NUMBERS DISCONTINUED

Date	Mintage	Fine	V.F.	E.F.	Unc/abt FDC
1879	Included above	£2	£9	£25	£50/ ---
1879	A proof	---	---	---	£125
1880	Hair lock on cheek	£3	£10	£30	£60/ ---
1880	No lock of hair ★	£2	£6	£15	£30/ £50
1880	No lock of hair ★ ★	(Colin Cooke 1991) abt.BU			---/ £50
	★ ★ The reverse of this example has smaller lettering than ★				
1880	A proof	---	---	---	£125
1881	6,239,447	£2	£6	£20	£40/ £60
1881	A proof	---	---	---	£150
1882	759,809	£3	£12	£36	£72/ ---
1883	4,986,558	£2	£6	£12	£25/ £40
1884	3,422,565	£2	£6	£15	£25/ £40
1884	Pattern bearing national emblems	---	---	---	£300
1885	4,652,771	£2	£6	£9	£15/ £25
1886	2,728,249	£2	£6	£10	£20/ £40
1886	A proof	---	---	---	£125
1887	3,675,607 Young Head	£2	£5	£10	£20/ £30
1887	A proof Young Head	---	---	---	£120

First Young Head 1838 to 1860 inclusive.
Second Young Head 1867 to 1880; as first but lower relief.
Third Young Head 1880 to 1887; Reverse has larger letters.

VICTORIA　Jubilee Head

Date	Mintage	Fine	V.F.	E.F.	abt. Unc/FDC

Reverse --A-- GARTERED SHIELD 'WITHDRAWN':

Date	Mintage	Fine	V.F.	E.F.	abt. Unc/FDC
1887	3,675,607	£1	£2	£5	£8/£15
1887	R of Victoria struck over V (or I)	--	---	---	£20/£30
1887	Proof Gartered Shield		--	---	£50/£75

Being the same size and design as the half-sovereign many were gold plated and passed as such. This led to the withdrawal of this design of sixpence.

1887	Pattern - Gartered Shield - date above crown				

Reverse --B-- CROWNED VALUE IN WREATH:

Date	Mintage	Fine	V.F.	E.F.	abt. Unc/FDC
1887	Included above	£1	£2	£4	£6/£10
1887	Proof Crowned Value In Wreath	---	---	---	£50/£75
1887	Patterns by Spink, Lion-Shield-Unicorn Reverse:				
	In gold, brass, copper, tin and aluminium.				
1888	4,197,698	£1	£3	£9	£15/£20
1888	A proof	---	---	---	£115
1889	8,738,928	£1	£3	£10	£20/£30
1890	9,386,955	£1	£4	£14	£28/£42
1890	A proof	---	---	---	£115
1891	7,022,734	£1	£3	£12	£24/£30
1892	6,245,746	£1	£3	£10	£20/£30
1893	7,350,619 Jubilee Head	£65	£175	£500	£750/£1200

OLD or WIDOW HEAD

Date	Mintage	Fine	V.F.	E.F.	abt. Unc/FDC
1893	Included above	£1	£2	£9	£18/£25
1893	A proof	---	---	£25	£40/£60
1894	3,467,704	£1	£3	£12	£22/£34
1895	7,024,631	£1	£3	£9	£18/£26
1896	6,651,699	£1	£3	£9	£18/£26
1897	5,031,498	£1	£3	£9	£18/£26
1898	5,914,100	£1	£3	£10	£20/£30
1899	7,996,804	£1	£3	£9	£18/£26
1900	8,984,354	£1	£3	£7	£14/£21
1901	5,108,757	£1	£3	£7	£14/£21

The sixpence became known as a "TANNER". The cab fare from the City of London to Tanner's Hill cost sixpence i.e. "A Tanner One".

A　　　　B

EDWARD VII　CROWNED SIXPENCE WITHIN WREATH 19mm

Date	Mintage	Fine	V.F.	E.F.	abt. Unc/FDC
1902	6,367,378	£1	£2	£8	£10/£18
1902	15,123 proofs with matt finish	--	---		FDC £14
1903	5,410,096	£1	£5	£15	£40/£60
1904	4,487,098	£2	£8	£25	£60/£85
1904	Noted 1994	"Toned UNC"	---		£75
1905	4,235,556	£2	£8	£22	£50/£70
1906	7,641,146	£1	£3	£14	£30/£40
1907	8,733,673	£1	£4	£16	£30/£45
1908	6,739,491	£1	£7	£21	£45/£65
1909	6,584,017	£1	£4	£15	£35/£50
1910	12,490,724	£1	£3	£9	£12/£25

GEORGE V　LION ON CROWN　19mm

Date	Mintage	Fine	V.F.	E.F.	abt. Unc/FDC
1911	9,155,310	---	£1.50	£7	£10/£15
1911	6,007 proofs	---	---	---	£22/£30
1912	10,984,129	---	£2	£12	£24/£36
1913	7,499,833	---	£3	£12	£24/£36
1914	22,714,602	---	£1	£5	£9/£15
1915	15,694,597	---	£1	£5	£9/£15
1916	22,207,178	---	£1	£5	£9/£15
1917	7,725,475	---	£2	£12	£24/£36
1918	27,558,743	---	£1	£6	£10/£15
1919	13,375,447	---	£1	£8	£18/£25
1920	14,136,287:				
	Silver .925	---	£2	£9	£18/---
	Silver .500	---	£1.50	£8	£15/£24
1921	30,339,741	---	£1	£6	£12/£24
1922	16,878,890	---	£1	£7	£15/£24
1923	6,382,793	---	£3	£15	£25/£40
1924	17,444,218	---	£1	£5	£10/£15
1925	12,720,558	---	£1	£5	£10/£15
1925	With new broader rim	---	£1.50	£9	£18/£25
1925	A pattern of the 1928 design in nickel				---
1926	21,809,261	---	£1	£8	£12/£18
1926	Modified Effigy (page 23)	£1	£3	£8	£9/£15
1927	68,939,873	£1	£2	£5	£12/£20
1927	15,000 proofs - Rev. new OAK/ACORN design				
1928	23,123,384	---	50p	£5	£9/£12
1929	28,319,326	---	50p	£3	£5/ £9
1930	16,990,289	---	60p	£3	£7/£10
1931	16,873,268 ★	---	75p	£5	£8/£12
1931	A proof	---	---	---	£175
1932	9,406,117 ★	---	75p	£4	£8/£14
1933	22,185,083	---	50p	£3	£5/ £8
1933	A proof	---	---	---	£180
1934	9,304,009	---	60p	£4	£7/£12
1935	13,995,621	---	50p	£3	£6/ £8
1936	24,380,171	---	30p	£3	£4/ £6

★ these have a finer grained (milled) edge

Date	Mintage		Fine	V.F.	E.F.	Unc/ abt. FDC

EDWARD VIII (Duke of Windsor)

1937	SIX LINKED RINGS of ST.EDWARD			(1989)		£9,500

GEORGE VI   *50% SILVER, 50% ALLOY to 1946 - 19mm*

Date	Mintage		Fine	V.F.	E.F.	Unc/abt. FDC
1937	22,302,524		---	25p	£1.50	£3/ £5
1937	26,402	proofs	---	---	---	£3/ £5
1938	13,402,701		---	---	£3	£6/£12
1939	28,670,304		---	---	£1.50	
1940	20,875,196		---	---	£1.50	
1941	23,186,616		---	---	£1.50	
1942	44,942,785		---	---	£1	£3/ £4
1943	46,927,111		---	---	£1	£3/ £4
1944	37,952,600		---	---	£1	£2/ £3
1945	39,939,259		---	---	£1	£2/ £3
1946	43,466,407		---	---	£1	£2/ £3

CUPRO-NICKEL

1946	Proof, for new coinage, in cupro-nickel				---	---
1947	29,993,263		---	---	45p	£1/ £2
1948	88,323,540		---	---	65p	£1/ £3

Monogram GRI was changed to GRVI in 1949 when title IND: IMP: (INDAE IMPERATOR) - Emperor of India- was relinquished

1949	41,355,515		---	---	75p	£2/ £4
1950	32,741,955		---	---	65p	£2/ £6
1950	17,513	proofs	---	---	---	£3/ £5
1951	40,399,491		---	---	65p	£2/ £5
1951	20,000	proofs	---	---	---	£3/ £5
1952	1,013,477		50p	£1.50	£10	£20/£30

MODIFIED EFFIGY : In the absence of a direct comparison, the modified effigy (or modified head) can be distinguished by the initials which appear on the truncation of the neck. Before modification, the initials B.M. are placed near the centre of truncation. After modification they appear, *without stops*, well to the right thus: BM (not B.M.) The initials are those of the designer of the coin: Bertram Mackennal.

SIXPENCES

Date	Mintage	Fine	V.F.	E.F.	Unc/FDC
ELIZABETH II		NATIONAL EMBLEMS INTERTWINED			
1953	70,323,876	---	---	25p	65p/ £1
1953	40,000 proofs	---	---	---	£2/ £3
	BRITT: OMN: discontinued				
1954	105,241,150	---	---	35p	£2/ £4
1955	109,929,554	---	---	20p	£1/ £2
1956	109,841,555	---	---	20p	£1/ £2
1957	105,654,290	---	---	20p	£1/ £2
1958	123,518,527	---	---	65p	£2/ £3
1959	93,089,441	---	---	---	£1/ £2
1960	103,288,346	---	---	50p	£2/ £5
1961	115,052,017	---	---	50p	£2/ £5
1962	178,359,637	---	---	---	50p/ £1
1963	112,964,000	---	---	---	50p/ £1
1964	152,336,000	---	---	---	50p/ £1
1965	129,644,000	---	---	---	20p/50p
1966	175,696,000	---	---	---	20p/50p
1966	"Mule" with Commonwealth Portrait @ auction 1993				£396
1967	240,788,000	---	---	---	15p/45p
1970	750,476 proofs for LAST STERLING set				£1/ £2

Various 'pointings' have been noted (see page 33)

1953 ELIZABETH - ELIZABETH

1955 SIXPENCE - SIXPENCE

1964 and 1965 REGINA - REGINA

EIGHTPENCES and OCTORINOS

GEORGE V — ESC refers to Seaby's "The English Silver Coinage"

PATTERNS by HUTH — Central Star bears LEGS OF MAN

1913	ESC 1481A	Pattern for eightpence in copper		£300/ ----
	ESC 1481	OCTORINO	---	£450
		Noted (Seaby 1990) abt.FDC		£450
1913	ESC 1482	EIGHTPENCE In silver	---	----/£450
	ESC 1482A	EIGHT PENCE in copper	---	----
		(Spink 1980) in iron		£225/ ---

These items appear only very rarely.

NINEPENCES

Date			V.F.	E.F.	Unc/FDC
GEORGE III Bank Token					Silver 22mm
1812	Pattern bank token.				
	Rev has BANK TOKEN 9D and the date in wreath of Oak and Olive:				
	(ESC 1478)		---	£375	£600/£850
1812	As above (ESC 1479) In copper		---	£400	£650/£900
1812	As above (ESC 1480) silver 9 PENCE		---		£700/£950

TENPENCES

VICTORIA One Franc — Silver 23mm

1867	Pattern - ESC 1416 ONE FRANC/TEN PENCE	£350	£700/£950

"Gothic" Head

Young Head

Jubilee Head

"Bun" Head

Old, Veiled, or Widow Head

GILLICK
(Mary Gillick)

MACHIN
(Arnold Machin)

MAKLOUF
(Raphael Maklouf)

Briefly: specially struck silver coins are distributed to as many old men and women as the Monarch has years; those years being 'expressed' in pence. Thus, on the Monarch's fortieth birthday, 40 men and 40 women each receive 40 pence or four Maundy sets at tenpence per set. The following year the distribution would be to 41 men and 41 women: four sets plus an extra penny. There are additonal sums, paid in conventional notes and coins, in lieu of food and clothing. The distribution takes place on Maundy Thursday: the day before Good Friday.

MAUNDY SETS

SILVER   FACE VALUE TEN PENCE   THE SET OF FOUR COINS

Date		Fine	V.F.	abt. E.F./Unc.
GEORGE III				
1763		£25	£50	£100/£150
1763	A proof set of utmost rarity	- - -		- - -
1765	Rarity equals that of 1763 proof			- - -
1766		£25	£50	£100/£150
1772	noted (2d 7 over 6; 4d 2 over 0)			abt.EF £100
1780		£25	£50	£100/£150
1784		£25	£50	£100/£150
1786	(Seaby 1988)	GVF	£60	- - -
1792	★ WIRE MONEY	£55	£100	£150/£250
1795	Return to normal numbering	£20	£30	£60/£90
1800		£20	£30	£60/£90
1817	'NEW' COINAGE • BULL HEAD	£40	£80	£120
1818		- - -	£40	£80/£120
1820		- - -	£40	£80/£120

★ WIRE MONEY is so called because of the thin, 'wiry' script used for the figures   1, 2, 3, 4.

(Above) 1792 "WIRE MONEY"

GEORGE IV

FACE VALUE TEN PENCE   THE SET OF FOUR COINS   abt.

Date		V.F.	E.F.	Unc./FDC
1822		£30	£60	£90/£120
1822	A proof set (ESC 2426)	---	---	£150
1823		£25	£50	£75/£100
1824		£30	£80	£125/£140
1825 to 1828		£25	£50	£75/£100
1828	A proof set (ESC 2433)	---	---	£150
1829		£25	£50	£75/£100
1830		£25	£50	£75/£100
1830	Noted 1989	(Saltford Coins) "Choice FDC"		£98

WILLIAM IV   Silver as illustrated

Date	V.F.	E.F.	abt. FDC from/to	Date	V.F.	E.F.	abt. FDC from/to
1831	£35	£80	£130/£200	1834	£35	£80	£130/£200
1831	Proof		£100/£250	1835	£35	£80	£120/£150
1831	Proof in gold		----	1836	£35	£80	£120/£150
1832	£35	£80	£120/£150	1837	£35	£80	£120/£150
1833	£35	£80	£120/£150				

MAUNDY ODDMENTS:

		V.F.	E.F.	Abt. Unc/FDC			V.F.	E.F.	Abt. Unc/FDC
1762	3d	£5	£10	---/---	1795	1d	---	£12	---/---
1765	2d	£225	---	---/---	1800	1d	---	£9	£15/---
1765	3d	---	£600	---/---	1800	2d	£5	£9	---/---
1766	2d	---	£15	---/---	1818	1d	---	---	---/£15
1779	1d	---	£25	---/---	1820	1d	---	£9	---/---
1780	2d	---	£9	---/---	1828	1d	---	£10	---/---
1781	1d	---	£25	---/---	1829	1d	---	£6	£9/---
1784	1d	---	£8	---/---	1831	1d	---	£10	---/---
1792	1d	---	£9	---/---	1832	4d	---	£20	---/---
1792	2d	£12	£25	---/---	1833	1d	---	£8	---/---
1792	3d	£15	£30	---/---	1834	1d	---	£9	---/---
1792	4d	£15	£30	---/---					

VICTORIA   *Young Head*

Date	Sets	EF.	abt Unc/FDC	Date	Sets	EF.	abt Unc/FDC
1838	4,158	£35	£50/£65	1871	4,488	£36	£50/£65
1838	Proofs	---	£115	1871	Proof Auct.89		£410
1838	Proofs in gold	---		1872	4,328	£36	£50/£65
1839	4,125	£35	£50/£70	1873	4,162	£36	£50/£65
1839	Proofs	---	£185	1874	4,488	£36	£50/£65
1840	4,125	£35	£50/£65	1875	4,154	£36	£50/£65
1841	2,574	£35	£50/£65	1876	4,488	£36	£50/£65
1842	4,125	£35	£50/£65	1877	4,488	£36	£50/£65
1843	4,158	£35	£50/£65	1878	4,488	£36	£50/£65
1844	4,158	£35	£50/£65	1878	Proofs	£50	£200
1845	4,158	£35	£50/£65	1879	4,488	£36	£50/£65
1846	4,158	£35	£50/£65	1880	4,488	£36	£50/£65
1847	4,158	£35	£50/£65	1881	Proofs	---	£200
1848	4,158	£35	£50/£65	1882	4,488	£36	£50/£65
1849	4,158	£42	£60/£75	1883	4,488	£36	£50/£65
1850	4,158	£35	£55/£70	1884	4,488	£36	£50/£65
1851	4,158	£35	£55/£70	1885	4,488	£36	£50/£65
1852	4,158	£35	£55/£70	1886	4,488	£36	£50/£65
1853	4,158	£35	£55/£70	1887	4,488	£40	£55/£75
1853	Proofs	---	£350/£500				
1854	4,158	£36	£50/£65		*Jubilee Head*		
1855	4,158	£36	£50/£65	1888	4,488	£36	£50/£65
1856	4,158	£36	£50/£65	1888	Proofs	---	---
1857	4,158	£36	£50/£65	1889	4,488	£45	£55/£70
1858	4,158	£36	£50/£65	1890	4,488	£45	£55/£70
1859	4,158	£36	£50/£65	1891	4,488	£45	£55/£70
1860	4,158	£36	£50/£65	1892	4,488	£45	£55/£70
1861	4,158	£36	£50/£65				
1862	4,158	£36	£50/£65		*Old or Widow Head*		
1863	4,158	£36	£50/£65	1893	8,976	£25	£35/£45
1864	4,158	£36	£50/£65	1894	8,976	£25	£35/£45
1865	4,158	£36	£50/£65	1895	8,877	£25	£35/£45
1867	4,158	£36	£50/£65	1896	8,476	£25	£35/£45
1867	Proofs		£265	1897	8,976	£20	£30/£40
1868	4,158	£36	£50/£65	1898	8,976	£25	£35/£45
1869	4,158	£36	£50/£65	1898	(1994) "FDC orig. case" £58		
1870	4,488	£36	£50/£65	1899	8,976	£25	£35/£45
				1900	8,976	£25	£35/£45
				1901	8,976	£25	£35/£45

Original Documentation Adds Value. Add £6/£9 for original dated case.

EDWARD VII

Date	Sets	EF.	F.D.C. from/to	Date	Sets	EF.	F.D.C. from/to
1902	8,976	£30	£40/£50	1906	8,800	£25	£35/£40
1902	15,123	matt proofs £40		1907	8,760	£25	£35/£40
1903	8,976	£25	£35/£40	1908	8,760	£25	£35/£40
1904	8,876	£25	£35/£40	1909	1,983	£35	£45/£55
1905	8,976	£25	£35/£40	1910	1,440	£40	£50/£60

GEORGE V

Date	Sets	EF.	Unc/FDC	Date	Sets	EF.	Unc/FDC
1911	1,768	£30	£40/£45	1924	1,515	£25	£35/£45
1911	proofs	---	£60	1925	1,438	£25	£35/£45
1912	1,246	£25	£35/£40	1926	1,504	£25	£35/£45
1913	1,228	£25	£35/£40	1927	1,647	£25	£35/£45
1914	982	£42	£50/£60	1928	1,642	£25	£35/£45
1915	1,293	£25	£35/£40	1929	1,761	£25	£35/£45
1916	1,128	£25	£35/£40	1930	1,724	£25	£35/£45
1917	1,237	£25	£35/£40	1931	1,759	£25	£35/£45
1918	1,375	£25	£35/£40	1932	1,835	£25	£35/£45
1919	1,258	£25	£35/£40	1933	1,872	£25	£35/£45
1920	1,399	£25	£35/£40	1934	1,887	£25	£35/£45
1921	1,386	£25	£35/£40	1935	1,928	£30	£45/£55
1922	1,373	£25	£35/£40	1936	1,323	£35	£50/£60
1923	1,430	£35	£45/£60			Orig. Documents Add Value	

MAUNDY ODDMENTS
(Virtually Mintlike)

	1d	2d	3d	4d		1d	2d	3d	4d
1822	£9	--	--	--	1902	--	£4	£12	--
1850	£6	--	--	£6	1903	£9	£10	--	---
1870	£5	--	--	--	1904	£9	£5	£9	£6
1880	£5	--	--	--	1905	£9	£9	£9	---
1888	£5	--	--	--	1911	--	--	--	£9
1898	--	--	--	£7	1912	£12	£9	£12	£12
1900	--	£4	--	--	1917	£12	£12	--	---

GEORGE VI

Date	Sets	abt Unc/FDC	Date	Sets	abt Unc/FDC
1937	1,325	£30/£40	1945	1,355	£30/£40
1938	1,275	£30/£40	1946	1,365	£30/£40
1939	1,234	£30/£40	1947	1,375	£30/£40
1940	1,277	£30/£40	1948	1,385	£30/£40
1941	1,253	£30/£40	1949	1,395	£30/£40
1942	1,231	£30/£40	1950	1,405	£30/£40
1943	1,239	£30/£40	1951	1,468	£30/£40
1944	1,259	£30/£40	1952	1,012	£40/£50

> 1937 to 1946 .500 silver was used.
> 1947 to 1952 a return to Sterling silver
> 1949 to 1952 a change of inscription
> 1952 Maundy was distributed by Queen Elizabeth.
> 1954 to 1970 a change of inscription.

ELIZABETH II

Date	Complete Sets		Unc/FDC
1953	1,025	St.Paul's Cathedral	£195/£225
1953	In gold	--- (1985)	£5,750
1954	1,020	Westminster Abbey	£35/£45
1955	1,036	Southwark Cathedral	£35/£45
1956	1,088	Westminster Abbey	£35/£45
1957	1,094	St.Alban's Cathedral	£35/£45
1958	1,100	Westminster Abbey	£40/£50
1959	1,106	Windsor	£40/£50
1960	1,112	Westminster Abbey	£40/£50
1961	1,118	Rochester Cathedral	£40/£50
1962	1,125	Westminster Abbey	£40/£50
1963	1,131	Chelmsford	£40/£50
1964	1,137	Westminster	£40/£50
1965	1,143	Canterbury	£40/£50
1966	1,206	Westminster	£40/£50
1967	986	Durham	£40/£50
1968	964	Westminster	£40/£50
1969	1,002	Selby	£40/£50
1970	980	Westminster	£40/£50
1971	1,018	Tewkesbury Abbey	£40/£50
1972	1,026	York Minster	£45/£55
1973	1,004	Westminster	£45/£55
1974	1,042	Salisbury	£45/£55

ELIZABETH II

Date	Complete Sets		Unc./ FDC
1975	1,050	Peterborough	£45/£55
1976	1,158	Hereford	£45/£55
1977	1,138	Westminster	£45/£55
1978	1,178	Carlisle	£40/£50
1979	1,189	Winchester	£40/£50
1980	1,198	Worcester	£40/£50
1981	1,208	Westminster	£40/£50
1982	1,218	St.David's Cathedral	£40/£50
1983	1,218	Exeter Cathedral	£40/£50
1984	1,243	Southwell Minster	£40/£50
1985	1,248	Ripon Cathedral	£40/£50
1986	1,378	Chichester Cathedral	£50/£60
1987	1,390	Ely Cathedral	£50/£60
1988	1,402	Lichfield Cathedral	£50/£60
1989	1,353	Birmingham Cathedral	(63p)	£50/£60
1990	1,523	St. Nicholas Newcastle	(64p)	£50/£60
1991	1,384	Westminster	(65p)	£50/£60
1992		Chester	(66p)	£50/£60
1993		Winchester	(67p)	£75/£85
1994		Truro Cathedral	(68p)	
1995			(69p)	

Averages of Maundy Sets are influenced by V.A.T.
Thus: a set was reported as 'at auction' £65
Investigation showed £65 + Buyer's Premium of
10%, + VAT on the whole - a total of £82.23

SHILLINGS

GEORGE III

Silver - 26 mm until 1816, then 23 mm

Date	Mintage/etc		Fine	V.F.	E.F.	abt Unc/FDC
1763	Northumberland		£100	£250	£350	----
1763	Noted 1994	(KB Coins) "gd EF"			£474	----
1764	Pattern (ESC1238)			(Spink 1988)	as struck £650	
1778	A pattern (ESC 1240)			---	£575	----
1786	Proof only		---	---	---	----
1787	No semee of hearts	£2	£10	£25	£40/£50	
1787	' ' ' ' no stop overhead		£12	£50	£70/£125	
1787	' ' ' ' no stops at date		£12	£55	£75/£150	
1787	Hearts in shield	£2	£10	£25	£40/£50	
1798	Dorrien & Magens, no stop o/hd (Seaby)		---			£4,000
1816	BULL HEAD 23 mm	£2	£4	£16	£25/£35	
1817	23,031,360	£1	£4	£18	£30/£45	
1817	GEOE (R over E)	£15	£45	£120	£165/---	
1818	1,342,440	£4	£15	£60	£75/£105	
1818	Second 8 higher	£6	£28	£100	£160/---	
1819	7,595,280	£2	£6.50	£32	£45/---	
1819	9 struck over 8	---	£15	£45	£90/---	
1819	Noted (Messrs. Weeks 1989 toned gem unc £150)					
1820	7,975,440	£2	£10	£30	£45/£75	

GEORGE IV

Laureate Head to 1925; Bare Head from L.o.C.
Rev. SHIELD:

Gnd = Garnished,   Gtd = Gartered.   23mm   L.o.C. = Lion on Crown

Date	Mintage/etc		Fine	V.F.	E.F.	abt Unc/FDC
1820	Pattern	Gnd (rarity 5)		(1986)		£2,012
1821	2,463,120	Gnd £3		£12	£40	£60/£100
1821	A proof	Gnd ---		---	---	£400/---
1823	693,000	Gtd £9		£35	£100	£200/---
1823	Noted 1994	(KB Coins)	"FDC toned"			£425
1823	A proof	Gtd ---		---	---	£800
1824	4,158,000	Gtd £3		£12	£35	£55/£75
1825	2,459,160	Gtd £3		£12	£35	£55/£75
1825	5 struck over 3 Gtd			---	---	----
1825	LION on CROWN rev.	£2	£6	£30	£50/£90
1826	6,351,840	L.o.C. £2		£6	£25	£40/£65
1826	6 struck over a 2nd 2	L.o.C.			---	----
1826	A proof	L.o.C. (ESC 1258)		---	FDC £200	
1827	574,200	L.o.C. £4		£25	£90	£140/£165
1829	879,120	L.o.C. £4		£15	£60	£80/£125

Date	Mintage	Fair / Fine	V.F.	E.F.	Unc/ abt FDC
WILLIAM IV	SILVER 23mm				
1831	Proofs, plain edge, from set		£135	£250/£350	
1834	3,223,440 grained edge £2.5	£10	£62	£120/£185	
1834	A proof with flat topped '3'	(1983)		FDC £600	
1835	1,449,360	£3	£12	£65	£125/£190
1836	3,567,960	£3	£10	£50	£70/£120
1837	479,160	£3	£22	£80	£175/----
1837	A proof	---	---	(1984)	£300
VICTORIA	SILVER 23mm				
1838	1,956,240 1st Head £3	£10	£30	£50/ £80	
1838	Noted 1994 (J. Welsh)	"Gem Unc. nice tone"		£85	
1838	Proofs	---	---	---	£300
1839	5,666,760	£3	£12	£40	£60/ £90
1839	Proof (with W.W.) from the sets	2nd Head		£250	
1839	No W.W. at neck	£1	£12	£45	£75/ £95
1839	Proof (no W.W.) grained edge	---		£750	
1840	1,639,440	£3 / £6	£20	£85	£125/£200
1841	875,160	£3 / £6	£20	£75	£125/£200
1842	2,094,840	£5	£10	£40	£60/ £90
1843	1,465,200	£4	£18	£60	£90/£125
1844	4,466,880	£2	£12	£50	£85/ ---
1845	4,082,760	£2	£14	£35	£50/ £95
1846	4,031,280	£2	£14	£35	£50/ £95
1848	1,041,480 (∗)	£20	£62	£200	£300/ ---
1849	645,480	£2	£12	£50	£95/£150
1850	685,080	£90	£300	£925	£1,500
1850	50 over 49	---	---	£1500	/ ---
1851	470,071	£15 / £30	£75	£250	£450/ ---
1852	1,306,574	£2	£12	£50	£75/ £95
1853	4,256,188	£2	£12	£50	£75/ £95
1853	Proofs from the sets	---		£300/£500	

(∗) 1848 all 8 struck over 6

Date	Mintage	Fine	V.F.	E.F.	Unc/ abt FDC
VICTORIA	SILVER 23mm				
1854	552,414	£30	£90	£200	£400/ ---
1855	1,368,499	£2	£12	£40	£70/ £85
1856	3,168,000	£2	£12	£40	£70/ £85
1857	2,562,120	£2	£12	£40	£70/ £85
1857	REG F: 9: (error inverted G)			£165	----
1858	3,108,600	£2	£12	£40	£70/ £85
1859	4,561,920	£2	£12	£30	£50/ £70
1860	1,671,120	£3	£20	£60	£100/£160
1861	1,382,040	£3	£20	£60	£125/£185
1861	1 over tilted I	(1988 near E.F. £45)			---
1862	954,360	£6	£40	£90	£135/£200
1863	859,320	£6	£40	£90	£150/£245
	THE FOLLOWING HAVE A DIE NUMBER (above date)				
1864	4,518,360	£2	£12	£40	£75/£115
1865	5,619,240	£2	£12	£40	£75/£115
	--- (ESC 1398) Undated pattern Seaby 1988 aFDC £650				
1866	4,989,600	£2	£12	£30	£60/ £90
1866	Noted 1994 (Weeks) "Gem, BU/FDC proof-like"				£125
1866	BBITANNIAR error	---	---		----
1867	2,166,120	£2	£12	£40	£70/£120
1867	Proof without Die No.	---	---		----
1867	Large head, lower relief 3rd Head			£200	£275/---
1868	3,330,360	£2	£12	£40	£90/£125
1869	736,560	£3	£15	£50	£100/£150
1870	1,467,471	£2	£14	£60	£100/£150
1871	4,910,010	£2	£9	£30	£50/ £75
1872	8,897,781	£2	£9	£25	£50/ £75
1873	6,489,598	£2	£8	£35	£60/ £90
1874	5,503,747	£2	£8	£35	£60/ £90
1875	4,353,983	£2	£8	£20	£40/ £65
1876	1,057,487	£2	£12	£35	£90/£125
1877	2,980,703	£2	£7	£25	£50/ £75
1878	3,127,131	£2	£7	£20	£40/ £65
1879	3,611,507	£5	£20	£60	£80/£120
1879	6 over 8 (Die 13)	(Numis. Circ.)			May, 1983

VICTORIA   Young Head   DIE NUMBER DISCONTINUED

Date	Mintage	Fine	V.F.	E.F.	Unc/abt FDC
1879	Included page 29	£3	£12	£50	£90/ ---
1880	4,842,786	£2	£7	£25	£48/£75
1881	5,255,332	£2	£7	£25	£45/£70
1881	Shorter line below SHILLING		£7	£25	£45/£70
1882	1,611,786	£5	£25	£80	£150/ ---
1883	7,281,450	£2	£6	£15	£40/£55
1884	3,923,993	£2	£7	£15	£30/£45
1885	3,336,527	£2	£7	£18	£35/£50
1886	2,086,819	£1	£5	£14	£35/£50
1887	4,034,133 Young head	£3	£12	£36	£50/£86

Jubilee Head

Date	Mintage	Fine	V.F.	E.F.	Unc/abt FDC
1887	Included above Rev. B	75p	£2	£5	£8/£12
1887	Rev. A	£3	£6	£18	£24/£36
1887	1,084 proofs from the sets	---	---		£50/£75
1888	Last 8 over 7	£3	---	---	---
1888	4,526,856	£1.50	£3	£15	£25/£40
1889	7,039,628 but ★	£10	£45	£200	£365/ ---
1889	★ Larger head	£2	£3.50	£15	£30/£60
1890	8,794,042	£2	£4	£20	£40/£60
1891	5,665,348	£2	£4	£20	£35/£55
1892	4,591,622	£1	£4	£26	£45/£65

Proofs exist for other dates but are rarely offered.
Messrs. Seaby's "The English Silver Coinage" lists some 40 patterns.

VICTORIA   Old, Veiled or Widow Head

THREE SHIELDS within GARTER - SILVER - 23mm

Date	Mintage	Fair/Fine	V.F.	E.F.	Unc/abt FDC
1893	7,039,074	£2	£3	£9	£20/£40
1893	Obv. small letters	--	£6	£18	£40/£60
1893	1,312 proofs from the sets				£45/£65
1894	5,953,152	£2	£4	£16	£30/£48
1895	8,880,651	£2	£4	£16	£30/£45
1896	9,264,551	£2	£3	£15	£25/£40
1897	6,270,364	£2	£3	£14	£22/£38
1898	9,768,703	£2	£3	£15	£25/£40
1899	10,965,382	£2	£3	£12	£20/£32
1900	10,937,590	£2	£3	£10	£18/£30
1901	3,426,294	£2	£3	£12	£20/£35

EDWARD VII   Reverse: LION on CROWN - SILVER 23mm

Date	Mintage	Fair/Fine	V.F.	E.F.	Unc/abt FDC
1902	7,809,481	£1	£2	£8	£15/£25
1902	Noted (Messrs Weeks 1989 Toned Gem Unc £23)				
1902	15,123 proofs matt finish			£5	£15/£25
1903	2,061,823	£2	£9	£35	£60/£95
1904	2,040,161	£2	£9	£30	£60/£95
1905	488,390	£18/£25	£75	£250	£500/ ---
1906	10,791,025	£1.50	£3	£18	£30/£50
1907	14,083,418	£1.50	£3	£12	£30/£50
1908	3,806,969	£2.50	£9	£40	£60/£95
1909	5,664,982	£2	£5	£40	£60/£100
1910	26,547,236	£1	£3	£10	£20/£30

> 1887 "shuttlecock" varieties : embellishment divides date · 18 87
> The device points to a rim tooth = Reverse A   Rare
> The device points between two teeth = Reverse B   Common

GEORGE V
Reverse: Lion-on-Crown · Date Divided · Inner Circle
SILVER (.925 to 1919 - .500 from 1920)   23mm

Date	Mintage	Fine	V.F.	E.F.	Unc/abt FDC
1911	20,065,901	---	£2	£6	£10/£16
1911	6,007 proofs	---	---	---	£28/£35
1912	15,594,009	---	£3	£18	£30/£50
1913	9,011,509	£2	£5	£26	£45/£70
1914	23,415,843	---	£2	£6	£10/£16
1915	39,279,024	---	£2	£4	£9/£14
1916	35,862,015	---	£2	£5	£10/£16
1917	22,202,608	---	£2	£6	£12/£18
1918	34,915,934	---	£2	£6	£10/£16
1919	10,823,824	---	£2	£9	£20/£30
	SILVER REDUCED to .500				
1920	22,825,142	---	£2	£9	£20/£30
1921	22,648,763	---	£3	£15	£25/£40
1922	27,215,738	---	£2	£10	£20/£30
1923	14,575,243	---	£2	£10	£20/£30
1923	Trial Piece in nickel	---	---	£200	£400
1924	Trial in nickel	---	---	£200	£400
1924	9,250,095	45p	£2.50	£12	£18/£35
1925	A pattern in nickel	---	---	---	
1925	Pattern in lead - obverse has the word MODEL - NVF £175 (1990)				
1925	5,418,764	£1	£5	£20	£36/£62
1926	22,516,453	45p	£2.50	£12	£20/£36
1926	Modified Effigy	---	£2.50	£8	£20/£32
1927	9,262,344	---	£2.50	£8	£22/£32

Obverse 1 = above B.M. the neck is hollow.   Reverse A = GEORGIVS

Obverse 2 = above B.M. the neck is flat.   Reverse B = GEORGIVS

1911 Varieties : 1 + A; 1 + B; 2 + A; 2 + B.
1912 Varieties : IMP closely spaced; I M P widely spaced.
1920 Varieties : Obverse 1; Obverse 2.

GEORGE V
Lion-on-Crown · Date at right · No inner circle
50% SILVER - 50% ALLOY

Date	Mintage	Fine	V.F.	E.F.	abt. Unc/FDC
1927	NEW DESIGN	---	£1.50	£6	£18/£25
1927	15,000 proofs	---	---	---	£18
1928	18,136,778	---	65p	£4	£7/£12
1929	19,343,006	---	65p	£4	£8/£12
1930	3,137,092	---	£3	£12	£24/£36
1931	6,993,926	---	75p	£5	£9/£15
1932	12,168,101	---	75p	£5	£9/£15
1933	11,511,624	---	65p	£4	£6/£10
1934	6,138,463	---	£2	£10	£20/£30
1935	9,183,462	---	65p	£4	£6/£10
1936	11,910,613	---	50p	£3	£5/£9

EDWARD VIII   (Duke of Windsor)
1936 a few Scottish but no English   ---   £12,000

GEORGE VI
50% SILVER/50% ALLOY until 1947

Date	Mintage	Fine	V.F.	E.F.	abt. Unc/FDC
1937E	8,359,122	---	---	£2	£5/£6
1937E	26,402 proofs	---	---	---	£8
1937S	6,748,875	---	---	£2	£4/£5
1937S	26,402 proofs	---	---	---	£8
1938E	4,833,436	---	---	£4	£14/£18
1938S	4,797,852	---	---	£4	£12/£16
1939E	11,052,677	---	---	£1	£4/£6
1939S	10,263,892	---	---	£1	£4/£6
1940E	11,099,126	---	---	£1	£4/£6
1940S	9,913,089	---	---	£1	£4/£6
1941E	11,391,883	---	---	£1	£4/£6
1941S	8,086,030	---	---	£2	£5/£7
1942E	17,453,643	---	---	£1	£3/£4
1942S	13,676,759	---	---	£1	£3/£4
1943E	11,404,213	---	---	£1	£3/£4
1943S	9,824,214	---	---	£1	£3/£4
1944E	11,586,752	---	---	£1	£3/£4
1944S	10,990,167	---	---	£1	£3/£4
1945E	15,143,404	---	---	60p	£2/£3
1945S	15,106,270	---	---	60p	£2/£3
1946E	18,663,797 see note	---	---	50p	£2/£3
1946E	Pattern, proof, or trial in cupro-nickel	---	---	---	
1946S	16,381,501	---	---	50p	£2/£3
1947E	12,120,611	---	---	75p	£3/£4
1947S	12,282,223	---	---	£1	£4/£6
1948E	45,576,923	---	---	50p	£2/£4
1948S	45,351,937	---	---	50p	£2/£4

See note regarding bullion on page 33

SHILLINGS

Date	Mintage		Fine	V.F.	E.F.	Unc. from/to
GEORGE VI (continued)						
1949E	19,328,405		---	---	£1	£3/£5
1949S	21,243,074		---	---	£2	£4/£5
1950E	19,243,872		---	---	£1.50	£4/£5
1950E	17,513	proofs	---	---	---	£6/£7
1950S	14,299,601		---	---	£1.60	£5/£6
1950S	17,513	proofs	---	---	---	£6/£7
1951E	9,956,930		---	---	£1	£3/£5
1951E	20,000	proofs	---	---	---	£6/£7
1951S	10,961,174		---	---	£1	£5/£6
1951S	20,000	proofs	---	---	---	£6/£7
1952E		1 known outside Royal Collection		---		----

Suffix E = English; and S = Scottish. In 1937 these coins were struck
with English, and Scottish, symbols and were circulated, generally, throughout
the United Kingdom. The practice continued until 1966; and for 1970.

> Some Heraldic terms:
> RAMPANT - such as lion rampant, see reverse of 1953,
> STATANT GUARDANT - see left-hand 1937 and 1951 below.
> PASSANT GUARDANT - the three leopards, left-hand 1953.
> SEJANT GUARDANT - sitting, facing: right-hand 1937 and 1951 below.

Passant guardant is sometimes described as couchant (lying down), but
the raised paw indicates otherwise. The three leopards are still
referred to as such on old coinage, but on modern strikings are likely
to be referred to as three lions.

> 1946E   Reverse A IND   Reverse B IND   (see page 33)

SHILLINGS

Date	Mintage		Fine	V.F.	E.F.	Unc. from/to
ELIZABETH II				CUPRO-NICKEL 23mm		
1953E	41,942,894		---	---	30p	50p/£1.50
1953E	40,000	proofs	---	---		FDC £3/ £4
1953S	20,663,528		---	---	30p	60p/ £1
1953S	40,000	proofs	---	---		FDC £3/ £4
1954E	30,262,032	BRITT. OMN discontinued			45p	£1/ £3
1954S	26,771,735		---	---	36p	£1/ £3
1955E	45,259,908		---	---	36p	£1/ £2
1955S	27,950,906		---	---	36p	£3/ £6
1956E	44,907,008		---	---	£1	£6/£12
1956S	42,853,637		---	---	£1	£6/£12
1957E	42,774,217		---	---	25p	£2/ £4
1957S	17,959,988		---	---	£3	£10/£15
1958E	14,392,305		---	---	£3	£10/£15
1958S	40,822,557		---	---	25p	£1/ £2
1959E	19,442,778		---	---	25p	£1/ £2
1959S	1,012,988		15p	50p	£2	£10/£15
1960E	27,027,914		---	---	25p	£1/ £2
1960S	14,376,932		---	---	25p	£1/ £2
1961E	39,816,907		---	---	15p	£2/ £3
1961S	2,762,558		---	10p	75p	£3/ £6
1961S	A proof		offered in 1984		---	£200
1962E	36,704,379		---	---	---	50p/ £1
1962S	18,967,310		---	---	---	50p/ £1
1963E	44,714,000		---	---	---	50p/ £1
1963S	32,300,000		---	---	---	15p/30p
1964E	8,590,900		---	---	---	30p/50p
1964S	5,239,100		---	---	---	50p/75p
1965E	9,216,000		---	---	---	30p/75p
1965S	2,774,000		---	---	---	50p/ £1
1966E	15,005,000	includes 3,000 minted in 1967				25p/45p
1966S	15,607,000	includes 3,000 minted in 1967				25p/45p
1968	Decimal equivalent FIVE NEW PENCE Introduced					
1970E	750,476	proofs for LAST STERLING set				75p/ £1
1970S	750,476	proofs for LAST STERLING set				75p/ £1

EIGHTEEN PENCES

Date	Mintage	Fine	V.F.	E.F.	Unc/abt FDC
GEORGE III	**Bank Token**				**Silver 26 mm**
1811	Armoured Bust	£3	£9	£25	£35/£60
1811	Proof	--	--	£180	£250
1812	Armoured Bust	£3	£10	£26	£40/£65
1812	Laureate Head	£2	£9	£25	£40/£65
1812	Proof	---	---	£180	£250
1812	Proof with small lettering reverse	---	---	---	£400
1812	Proof in platinum	---	---	---	£500
1813	Laureate Head	£2	£9	£25	£40/£65
1813	Proof in platinum	---	---	---	£500
1814	Laureate Head	£2	£9	£25	£40/£65
1815	Laureate Head	£2	£9	£25	£40/£65
1816	Laureate Head	£2	£9	£25	£40/£65

'POINTINGS' are very much the key to some varieties. A principal feature such as a letter or ornament is selected and its 'attitude' is used to indicate the use of a different die-punch. Thus HALFPENNY (L̇) indicates that the upright of the 'L' is aimed *at* a rim bead. HALFPENNY (L̤) that 'L' points *between* two beads. Many dies are used to complete a full year's striking. New dies are usually identical being from the same, original punch. Differences are, therefore, interesting numismatically and unequal strikings must, eventually, show up in valuations.

NOTE ON BULLION VALUE. Although the collector's value of a worn coin is listed as face-value-only (---), a silver one may have a higher, bullion value because of the precious metal in it. At one time pre 1947 silver coins were worth 4 times face value and pre 1920 ones up to 7 or 8 times. Buyers now make quotations on a day-to-day basis. A large enough quantity to sell is necessary to offset the cost of mailing. Check rates on Teletext. Be sure to contact the dealer before sending.

★ Have varieties with no stop after date.   Rarity R2
+ Have varieties with no stop after date.   Rarity R
! With colon after date: 1865 R3;   1866   R2
1867 brit: is normal;   proofs/patterns have britt:
1874 has variety   'iv struck over iii'.   Rarity R2
1887 normal has 33 arcs;   variety 46 arcs.   Rarity R
R = rare;   R2 = very rare;   Seaby/Rayner scale.

FLORINS *Godless and Gothic*

		Fine	V.F.	E.F.	Unc/FDC abt
VICTORIA	**Silver 27 mm**				
1848	'GODLESS' (having no DEI GRATIA) patterns £300				£700
1848	As above but with grained (milled) edge	---			£2350
1849	413,830 'Godless'	£5	£18	£40	£65/£125
GOTHIC - date appears in Roman - third column - 30mm.					
1851	1,540 mdcccli	----	----	----	£2000
1852	1,014,552 mdccclii	£4	£16	£60	£120/£200
1852	ll struck over l (Messrs. Weeks 1993) abtEF £95				
1853 ★	3,919,950 mdcccliii	£4	£24	£80	£135
1853	Proof	----	----	----	£800
1854	550,413 mdcccliv	£200	£450	£1300	
1855	831,017 mdccclv	£5	£25	£82	£145/----
1856 ★	2,201,760 mdccclvi	£5	£26	£95	£160/----
1857	1,671,120 mdccclvii	£5	£25	£82	£140/£250
1857	Proof (ESC815)	----	----	----	£875
1858 +	2,239,380 mdccclviii	£4	£18	£70	£120/£175
1858	Noted (no stop after date Seaby 1989 EF/GEF £110)				----
1859 +	2,568,060 mdccclix	£4	£24	£80	£135/----
1860	1,475,100 mdccclx	£5	£30	£110	£180/----
1862	594,000 mdccclxii	£20	£80	£275	£400/----
1863	938,520 mdccclxiii	£30	£125	£450	£900/----
1864	1,861,200 mdccclxiv	£5	£25	£85	£145/----
1865 !	1,580,044 mdccclxv	£6	£30	£105	£175/----
1866 !	914,760 mdccclxvi	£6	£30	£105	£180/----
1867	423,720 mdccclxvii	£15	£60	£200	£340/----
1868	896,940 mdccclxviii	£5	£25	£82	£145/----
1869	297,000 mdccclxix	£4	£24	£80	£140/----
1870	1,080,648 mdccclxx	£4	£24	£80	£140/----
1871	3,425,605 mdccclxxi	£4	£24	£80	£140/----
1872	7,199,690 mdccclxxii	£4	£22	£70	£120/----
1873	5,921,839 mdccclxxiii	£4	£22	£70	£120/£190
1874	1,642,630 mdccclxxiv	£4	£24	£80	£140/----
1875	1,117,030 mdccclxxv	£4	£24	£80	£140/----
1876	580,034 mdccclxxvi	£5	£26	£100	£165/----
1877	682,292 mdccclxxvii	£5	£26	£100	£165/----
1877	No WW (48 arcs)	£15	£60	£200	----/----
1877	No WW (42 arcs)	£12	£50	£120	£190/----
1878	1,786,680 mdccclxxviii	£4	£24	£80	£140/----
1879	1,512,247 mdccclxxix				
Die No.	48 arcs WW (ESC849B) £30	£80		----	
No Die No.	42 arcs (ESC 850)	£20	£70	(no WW)	----
No Die No.	48 arcs WW (ESC 851)	£7	£25	£75	£165/----
No WW	38 arcs (ESC 852)	£6	£20	£65	£150/----
1880	2,167,170 mdccclxxx	£4	£24	£80	£140/----
1881	2,570,337 mdccclxxxi	£4	£22	£75	£125/----
1881	Broken die mdccclxxi	£4	£22	£75	£135/----
1883	3,555,667 mdccclxxxiii	£4	£22	£70	£115/----
1884	1,447,379 mdccclxxxiv	£4	£22	£70	£115/----
1885	1,758,210 mdccclxxxv	£4	£22	£75	£120/----
1886	591,773 mdccclxxxvi	£4	£22	£80	£135/----
1887	1,776,903 mdccclxxxvii	£7	£30	£130	£225/----

Those above are inscribed: **one tenth of a pound**
1887 See also 'Jubilee Head' on next page
Proofs exist for many dates; they are rare and rarely offered

Date	Mintage	Fair/Fine	V.F.	E.F.	Unc/abt. FDC.
VICTORIA	**Jubilee Head**				28 mm
1887	Incl page 33	£2	£4	£8	£12/£20
1887	1,084 Jubilee Head proofs			£45	£65/£80
1888	1,541,540	£2	£4	£15	£30/£50
1889	2,973,561	£2/£3	£5	£18	£35/£60
1890	1,684,737	£4	£15	£60	£85/£150
1891	836,438	£6	£25	£75	£115/£185
1892	283,401	£12	£40	£85	£140/£200
	Old, Veiled or Widow Head				
1893	1,666,103	£1.50	£6	£25	£45/£70
1893	1,312 proofs	- - -	- - -	- - -	- - -/£125
1894	1,952,842	£2	£8	£30	£45/£75
1895	2,182,968	£2	£7	£28	£40/£65
1896	2,944,416	£2	£7	£28	£40/£65
1897	1,699,921	£2/£3	£4	£25	£40/£60
1898	3,061,343	£2	£4	£25	£40/£60
1899	3,966,953	£2	£4	£25	£40/£55
1900	5,528,630	£2	£4	£25	£40/£55
1901	2,648,870	£2	£4	£24	£40/£55
1911	Two obverses (see page 10)				
1914	Large rim teeth and small rim teeth				
1920	BRĪTT and BRITT				

FLORINS (Two Shillings)

Date	Mintage	Fine	V.F.	E.F.	abt. Unc/FDC.
EDWARD VII		**Britannia standing**		Silver 28 mm	
1902	2,189,575	£3	£9	£25	£40/£65
1902	15,123 matt finished proofs			- - -	£20/£45
1903	1,995,298	£4	£12	£35	£55/£90
1904	2,769,932	£5	£15	£50	£100/£150
1905	1,187,596	£14	£45	£160	£300/£460
1906	6,910,128	£3	£10	£40	£80/£120
1907	5,947,895	£3	£10	£40	£90/£140
1908	3,280,010	£4	£14	£70	£140/£200
1909	3,482,289	£4	£14	£70	£140/£200
1910	5,650,713	£2	£8	£40	£80/£120
GEORGE V		From 1920 silver reduced to 50%			
		Shields/Sceptres in Quarters			
1911	5,951,284	- - -	£4	£18	£30/ £45
1911	6,007 proofs	- - -	- - -	- - -	£40/ £50
1912	8,571,731	- - -	£5	£28	£45/ £75
1913	4,545,278	- - -	£5	£30	£45/ £75
1914	21,252,701	- - -	£2	£9	£16/ £28
1915	12,367,939	- - -	£2	£10	£15/ £25
1916	21,064,337	- - -	£2	£9	£15/ £25
1917	11,181,617	- - -	£3	£12	£20/ £30
1918	29,211,792	- - -	£2	£7	£14/ £21
1919	9,469,292	- - -	£3	£11	£20/ £32
1920	15,387,833	(.500 silver)	£3	£15	£30/ £45
1921	34,863,895	£2	£3	£7	£18/ £25
1922	23,861,044	£2	£5	£9	£20/ £30
1923	21,546,533	£2	£6	£12	£25/ £38
1924	4,582,372	£2	£5	£20	£40/ £60
1925	1,404,136	£5	£12	£70	£135/£210
1925	Uniface pattern in lead (Seaby 1990) VF+ £225				

FLORINS (Two Shillings)

Date	Mintage	Fine	V.F.	E.F.	Unc/ abt. FDC
GEORGE V		(continued)			
1926	5,125,410	£2	£4	£20	£40/ £65
1927	15,000	proofs of new design	---	---	£35/ £50
1928	11,087,186	£2	£3	£6	£10/ £15
1929	16,397,279	£2	£4	£7	£10/ £15
1930	5,753,568	£2	£4	£6	£12/ £18
1931	6,556,331	£2	£4	£6	£10/ £18
1932	717,041	£3	£15	£60	£120/£180
1933	8,685,303	£2	£3	£6	£10/ £18
1934	none	---	---	---	---/ ---
1935	7,540,546	£2	£3	£7	£10/ £18
1936	9,897,448	£2	£4	£8	£12/ £20
EDWARD VIII	as GEORGE VI but monogram ER				
GEORGE VI		50/50 silver/alloy until 1947 - 28 mm			
1937	13,006,781	---	---	£2	£3/ £5
1937	26,402	proofs ---	---	---	£8/ £10
1938	7,909,388	---	---	£5	£12/£16
1939	20,850,607	---	---	£3	£4/ £6
1939	Proof	---	(Spinks 1986)		/£165
1940	18,700,338	---	---	£2	£3/ £5
1941	24,451,079	---	---	£2	£3/ £5
1942	39,895,243	---	---	£2	£3/ £4
1943	26,711,987	---	---	£2	£3/ £4
1944	27,560,005	---	---	£2	£3/ £4
1945	25,858,049	---	---	£2	£2/ £3
1946	22,910,085	---	---	£2	£2/ £3
CUPRO-NICKEL					
1946	Trial Piece in cupro-nickel, for new coinage				---
1947	22,910,085	---	---	80p	£2/ £3
1948	67,553,636	---	---	70p	£2/ £3
1949	28,614,939	---	---	£1.50	£4/ £6
1949	Proof	---	---	---	£160/ ---
1950	24,357,490	---	---	£1.60	£4/ £6
1950	17,513	proofs ---	---	---	£8/ ---
1951	27,411,747	---	---	£1.65	£5/ £8
1951	20,000	proofs ---	---	---	£8/ --

Date	Mintage	Fine	V.F.	E.F.	abt. Unc/FDC
ELIZABETH II			Cupro-nickel		28 mm
1953	11,958,710	---	---	£1	£2/£4
1953	40,000	proofs	---	---	£4/£6
1954	13,085,422	---	---	£5	£20/£40
1955	25,887,253	---	---	60p	£1/£3
1956	47,824,500	---	---	60p	£2/£3
1957	33,071,282	---	---	£2	£12/£25
1958	9,564,580	---	---	£1	£6/£12
1958	Proof Noted 1993	" V.I.P. proof FDC"			£250
1959	14,080,319	---	---	£2	£12/£30
1960	13,831,782	---	---	50p	£1/£3
1961	37,735,315	---	---	50p	£1/£3
1962	35,147,903	---	---	30p	£1/£3
1963	25,562,000	---	---	20p	£1/£3
1964	16,539,000	---	---	20p	£1/£3
1965	48,163,000	---	---	20p	50p/£2
1966	84,041,000	---	---	20p	50p/£2
1967	22,152,000	---	---	20p	50p/£2
1968	17,566,000	dated 1967.	Decimals Introduced.		
1970	750,476	proofs for Last Sterling set			£2

Continued on page 45 under DECIMAL COINAGE

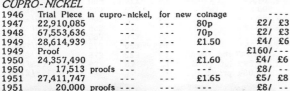

HALF DOLLARS

Date	Details	Fine	V.F.	E.F.
Half Dollars are Countermarked 4 reales				33 mm
Oval countermarks of George III		£60	£150	£300

PIECES OF FOUR, which is what these are, doesn't have the same 'ring' as PIECES OF EIGHT. Half Dollars are virtually identical to the coin shown on page 39 except 8R is replaced by 4R (or 4 to right of shield in some types) and, of course, the small difference in diameter. Apart from Reales, other large silver coins were used after being countermarked.

Date	Mintage	Fine	V.F.	E.F.	Unc/FDC
GEORGE III					Silver 32 mm
1816	Bull Head	£4	£16	£70	£100/£180
1816	Proof	---	---	---	£1,000
1817	8,092,656	£4	£16	£65	£95/£175
1817	Smaller head	£5	£20	£75	£120/£200
1817	D of DEI over T	--- (at auction 1987)			£325/----
1818	2,905,056	£6	£20	£70	£160/£200
1819	4,790,016	£6	£20	£70	£160/£200
1820	2,396,592	£8	£24	£90	£180/£250
	(inc 1820 George IV) Proofs exist for each date				
GEORGE IV					Silver 32 mm
1820	Garnished Shield	£4	£25	£85	£175/----
1821	1,435,104	£5	£26	£90	£175/£290
1821	Proof	---	---	£300	£525/£700
1822	Proof (only 2 known)	1993		FDC	£3,650
1823	2,003,760	£150	£500	£1800	£3,000
1823	Shield in Garter	£6	£25	£115	£130/£275
1823	Pattern (ESC 652)	1991		FDC	£4,800
1824	465,696 ?	£8	£35	£140	£225/£350
1824	Bare Head	£200	£750	£2650	----/----
1825	2,258,784	£7	£28	£80	£160/£200
1825	Proofs (ESC 643; and 644)				/£850
1825	Proof (ESC 645) in Barton's Metal : a sandwich of copper and two skins of gold.			(1984) £1,500	
1826	2,189,088	£6	£24	£96	£120/£216
1826	Proofs from the sets	---	£150		£250/£400
1828	49,890 ?	£10	£40	£175	£300/----
1829	508,464	£9	£36	£150	£265/£350
	Proofs except 1828 and 1829; patterns 1820/22/23/24				
	Pattern "Binfield" (ESC 655) 1991 abt.Unc.				£395/----
WILLIAM IV					Silver 32 mm
1831	Proofs from the sets (noted 1994 gdEF £295)				----/----
1834 ★	993,168 WW	£10	£40	£150	£275/£400
1834 ★	WW in script	£4	£24	£90	£200/£290
1835	281,952	£9	£40	£125	£200/£350
1836	1,588,752	£6	£24	£96	£120/£200
1836	6 struck over 5	£9	£45	£100	£150/£250
1837	150,526	£10	£40	£160	£200/£360
	1834 ★ proofs for both types of signature				

Date	Mintage	Fine	V.F.	E.F.	Unc./FDC
VICTORIA *Young Head*					Silver 32 mm
1839	Raised WW (at neck)		£600	£2250	ornamental fillets
1839	Incuse (struck in) WW		£550	£2000	plain hair fillets
1839	Proofs from the sets		---	£150	£300/£450
1840	386,496	£12	£50	£150	£300/£450
1841	42,768	£20	£85	£300	£600/----
1842	486,288	£7	£35	£100	£175/£275
1843	454,608	£16	£60	£200	£300/£450
1844	1,999,008	£6	£25	£90	£150/£240
1845	2,231,856	£6	£25	£90	£150/£240
1846	1,539,668	£6	£25	£90	£150/£240
1848	367,488 8/6	£30	£120	£360	£475/£650
1849	261,360 large date	£10	£50	£175	£250/£360
1849	Smaller date	£12	£55	£200	£275/£375
1850	484,613	£8	£42	£175	£350/----
1853	Proofs from the sets (ESC 687)		---		£1,500
1862	Proofs (ESC 688) and (ESC 689)		---		£2,500
1864	Proof only, for the Albert Memorial		---		£3,000
1874	2,188,599	£4	£20	£80	£160/£225
1875	1,113,483	£4	£22	£75	£145/----
1876	633,221	£4	£24	£80	£150/----
1876	6 struck over 5	---	---		----
1877	447,059	£4	£16	£65	£100/£150
1878	1,466,232	£4	£16	£65	£100/£150
1879	901,356	£5	£20	£80	£140/£220
1879	Proof (ESC704)		(Seaby 1990 abtFDC) £1100		
1880	1,346,350	£4	£20	£70	£110/£160
1881	2,301,495	£4	£14	£60	£100/£150
1882	808,227	£4	£25	£75	£125/£200
1883	2,982,779	£4	£16	£60	£120/----
1884	1,569,175	£4	£20	£65	£120/----
1885	1,628,438	£4	£20	£65	£120/----
1886	891,767	£4	£20	£75	£120/£200
1887	261,747 Yng. Head	£4	£22	£75	£120/£200
1887	1,176,299 Jub. Head	£2	£5	£9	£15/£25
1887	1,084 proofs	--	---		£125/£145

HALF CROWNS

Date	Mintage	Fine	V.F.	E.F.	Unc/abt. FDC
VICTORIA		Jubilee Head			(continued)
1888	1,428,787	£3	£6	£25	£40/£65
1889	4,811,954	£3	£5	£20	£30/£50
1890	3,228,111	£3	£10	£35	£50/£75
1891	2,284,632	£3	£10	£30	£55/£80
1892	1,710,946	£3	£10	£30	£50/£75
		Old or Widow Head			
1893	1,792,600	£2	£7	£20	£30/£50
1893	1,312 proofs	---	---		£110
1894	1,524,960	£3	£9	£40	£50/£70
1895	1,772,662	£3	£7	£30	£40/£60
1896	2,148,505	£3	£7	£30	£40/£60
1897	1,678,643	£3	£7	£25	£35/£55
1898	1,870,055	£3	£7	£30	£40/£60
1899	2,863,872	£3	£7	£30	£40/£60
1900	4,479,128	£3	£7	£20	£30/£50
1901	1,516,570	£3	£7	£20	£30/£50

Several patterns, proofs and varieties occur.

EDWARD VII   SILVER 32mm

Date	Mintage	Fine	V.F.	E.F.	Unc/abt. FDC
1902	1,316,008	£2	£6	£20	£30/£50
1902	15,123 matt surfaced proofs			---	£45/£65
1903	274,840	£20	£75	£225	£450/£625
1904	709,652	£9	£45	£200	£300/£400
1905	166,008	£65	£200	£700	£900/---
1906	2,886,206	£3	£8	£40	£75/£120
1907	3,693,930	£3	£9	£40	£75/£120
1908	1,758,889	£4	£15	£60	£95/£165
1909	3,051,592	£3	£12	£50	£80/£130
1910	2,557,685	£3	£9	£40	£70/£100

Proofs noted: 1890 £350; 1864 £825; 1876 £1,250.

HALF CROWNS

Date	Mintage	Fine	V.F.	E.F.	Unc/FDC
GEORGE V		SILVER to 1920; then 50/50 SILVER/ALLOY			
1911	2,914,573	---	£5	£20	£40/£60
1911	6,007 proofs				£60/£70
1912	4,700,789	---	£5	£25	£50/£75
1913	4,090,160	---	£7	£30	£60/£90
1914	18,333,003	---	---	£10	£20/£30
1915	32,433,066	---	---	£10	£20/£30
1916	29,530,020	---	---	£10	£15/£25
1917	11,172,052	---	£2	£12	£25/£35
1918	29,079,592	---	---	£7	£14/£22
1919	10,266,737	---	---	£15	£25/£36
	NOW REDUCED TO .500 SILVER				
1920	17,983,077			£15	£30/£45
1921	23,677,889	DEI and DEÏ (see page 33)		£15	£25/£40
1922	16,396,774	Rev.A = Crown on shield (thin groove)		£15	£30/£45
		Rev.B = Wide groove twixt crown and shield			
1923	26,308,526	---	---	£10	£16/£25
1924	5,866,294	---	---	£20	£40/£60
1925	1,413,461	£3	£15	£100	£150/£250
1926	4,473,516	---	---	£30	£45/£75
1926	No colon after OMN	£5	£25	£165	£260/----
1926	Modified Effigy (see page 23)	£4	£30		£50/£75
1927	6,852,872	---	---	£10	£20/£35
1927	15,000 proofs, new design	---		--	£20/£30
1928	18,762,727	---	---	£6	£10/£16
1929	17,632,636	---	---	£6	£10/£16
1930	809,501	£3	£10	£60	£120/£180
1931	11,264,468	---	---	£9	£15/£20
1932	4,793,643	---	---	£15	£30/£50
1933	10,311,494	---	---	£7	£14/£21
1934	2,422,399	---	---	£20	£30/£65
1935	7,022,216	---	---	£6	£10/£16
1935	A proof changed hands in 1975 for				£160/----
1936	7,039,423	---	---	£5	£10/£15

1928 Rosette: ★ = Rev. A; ★ = Rev. B   1929 Varieties as for 1928

Date	Mintage		Fine	V.F.	E.F.	Unc/ abt FDC
EDWARD VIII		*(Duke of Windsor)*				·500 SILVER
1937	Standard bearing Royal Arms (1993)					£16,000

GEORGE VI   .500 SILVER until 1947 - 32mm

Date	Mintage		Fine	V.F.	E.F.	Unc/abt FDC
1937	9,106,440		--	--	£2	£5/£7
1937	26,402	proofs	--	--	--	FDC £10
1938	6,426,478		--	£1	£3	£12/£17
1938	Noted 1994		"FDC superb"	--		£25
1939	15,478,635		--	--	£2	£5/£8
1940	17,948,439		--	--	£3	£6/£9
1941	15,773,984		--	--	£2	£5/£7
1942	31,220,090		--	--	£2	£4/£6
1943	15,462,875		--	--	£2	£5/£7
1944	15,255,165		--	--	£2	£3/£5
1945	19,849,242		--	--	£1	£3/£5
1946	22,724,873		--	--	£1	£3/£5

NOW CUPRO-NICKEL (no silver)

Date	Mintage		Fine	V.F.	E.F.	Unc/abt FDC
1947	21,911,484		--	--	£1	£2/£4
1948	71,164,703		--	--	£1	£2/£4
1949 ★	28,272,512		--	--	£1	£5/£8
1950	28,335,500		--	--	£1	£5/£7
1950	17,513	proofs	--	--	--	£6/£9
1951	9,003,520		--	--	£1.50	£4/£6
1951	20,000	proofs	--	--	--	£5/£8
1952	1 Sold by "Private Treaty" in 1991					£28,500

Date	Mintage		Fine	V.F.	E.F.	abt. Unc/FDC
ELIZABETH II					CUPRO-NICKEL 32mm	
1953	4,333,214	DEI ..	--	75p	£1.5/£2.5
1953	See page 33	DEI	--	80p	£2/£3
1953	40,000 proofs	--	--	--	£4/£6
1954	11,614,953	--	--	£4	£15/£25
1954	Proof	--	--	(1985)	/£225
1955	23,628,726	--	--	£1	£3/£5
1956	33,934,909	--	--	£1	£3/£5
1957	34,200,563	--	--	50p	£2/£4
1958	15,745,668	--	--	£3	£12/£20
1959	9,028,844	--	--	£4	£25/£30
1960	19,929,191	--	--	75p	£3/£4
1961	25,887,897	--	--	--	£1/£2
1962	24,013,312	--	--	--	£1/£2
1963	17,557,600	--	--	--	£1/£2
1964	5,973,600	--	--	50p	£2/£3
1965	9,878,400	--	--	--	£1/£2
1966	13,384,000	--	--	--	70p/£1.5
1967	18,895,200	--	--	--	45p/£1
1968	14,163,200 but dated 1967	--	--	--	
1969	Halfcrowns were demonetized 31st December.				
1970	Proofs from the 8-coin set	--	--		£2/£2.5

THREE SHILLINGS

GEORGE III   BANK OF ENGLAND TOKENS   SILVER 34/35mm
    VALUE and DATE enclosed by OAKWREATH: varying acorn count

Date	Description	Fine	V.F.	E.F.	Unc/FDC
1811	Acorns number 26	£5	£15	£40	£55/ £95
1811	Acorns numbering 24, 25, or 27; also proofs				----
1811	(ESC 410) obverse A2 + reverse with 26 acorns (1992)				/£500
1812	Armoured bust (ESC 415)	£5	£15	£40	£60/£100
1812	Laureate head (ESC 416)	£4	£12	£30	£45/ £75
1812	Obverse B1 (ESC 417) oak/olive wreath, proof				£475
1813	Similar to illustration	£4	£12	£35	£50/ £85
1814	Similar to illustration	£4	£12	£35	£50/ £85
1815	Similar to illustration	£4	£12	£35	£50/ £85
1816	Similar to illustration	£80	£165	£250	£350/£500

★ IND: IMP (Emperor of India)
   discontinued from 1949

(Four Shillings) DOUBLE FLORINS

Date	Mintage	Fine	V.F.	E.F.	abt. Unc/FDC
VICTORIA	Jubilee Head			SILVER 36mm	
1887	483,347 Roman I	£4	£8	£16	£22/£45
1887	Roman I proof	--	--	---	£150/£200
1887	Arabic 1 in date	£4	£8	£16	£22/£45
1887	Arabic 1 proof	--	--	---	£150/£200
1888	243,340	£5	£10	£25	£50/£85
1888 ★	Inverted 1 for second I	£6	£20	£55	£125/£180
1889	1,185,111	£4	£8	£16	£32/£50
1889 ★	Inverted 1 for second I	£7	£22	£65	£130/£195
1890	782,146	£5	£12	£25	£50/£75
1890	Pattern with reverse worded DOUBLE FLORIN				---

★ 2nd I of VICTORIA   J.E.B. at truncation = Designer/Engraver Joseph Boehm

GEORGE V

SILVER 36mm
1910 Double Florin in gold   ---   (1986)   £5,700
1911 Rare   Plain and grained edge patterns (sundry metals)
1911 As picture but DOUBLE FLORIN (1989 abtFDC £450)
1914 With the words TWELVE GROATS and in various metals

GEORGE VI

SILVER 36mm
1950 Patterns, grained edge,   George and Dragon   ext. rare
1950 As previous coin but 'FOUR SHILLINGS' struck into the edge

---

SILVER DOLLARS   (4/9d; 5/-; or 5/6d !)   39

(Face Value 4/9d: thus "Two King's Heads not worth a Crown")

Date	Fine	V.F.	E.F.	Unc.
GEORGE III				
COUNTERMARKED SPANISH 8 REALES				39/40mm
Oval mark from hallmark punch	£50	£100	£225	(ESC129)
Noted (Coin V.F. Cmk E.F. Spink 1988)	£150	----	----	(ESC129)
Noted (Coin nV.F. Cmk GVF Seaby 1990)	£120	----	----	(ESC129)
Octagonal mark from Maundy punch	£90	£175	£600	----
Oval mark on Louis XVI half-ECU	(1976)	£700		
1798 octagonal c/mk Fine	£190	(Grantham Coins 1993)		

A 'PIECE OF EIGHT' showing oval countermark

BANK OF ENGLAND DOLLARS

				Unc/FDC
1804	FIVE SHILLINGS (ESC 144)	£20	£80	£150	£200/£300
1804	(ESC 149)		GVF	£95	----
1804	Thick flan (similar ESC 165)	(1980)			£3000
PATTERNS:					
1804	Garter Dollar	(ESC 182)	(1993)	£850	----
1804	Garter Dollar	(ESC 185)	(1984)	----	£1500
1804	Garter Dollar	(ESC 186)	(1980)	----	£4000
1811	Oakwreath Dollar (ESC 206 5/6d)	(1983)	£600		

CROWNS (Five Shillings) SILVER 38mm

Date	Mintage		Fine	V.F.	E.F.	Unc/abt. FDC
GEORGE III		*Laureate Head · St. George/Dragon Reverse*				
1818	155,232	LVIII	£8	£25	£100	£140/£200
1818		LIX	£8	£25	£100	£140/£200
1819	683,496	LIX	£8	£25	£100	£140/£200
1819	9 over 8	LIX	£20	£70	£200	£400/£500
1819	No edge stops	LIX	£20	£75	£250	£450/£675
1819		LX	£8	£30	£95	£130/£175
1819	No stop after TUTAMEN		£12	£42	£160	£300/£450
1820	448,272	LX	£8	£30	£120	£180/£250
1820	20 over 19	LX	£15	£60	£130	£300/£450
1820	Undated pattern (ESC221) by Webb & Mills (1991)					£495

Patterns greatly prized. THE THREE GRACES (1980) £3,500
A set (3) (silver, tin, encapsulated tin) Spinks 1984 £12,500

CROWNS SILVER 38mm

Mintage		Fine	V.F.	E.F.	Unc/abt. FDC
GEORGE IV	*Laureate Head · St. George/Dragon Reverse*				
1820	Pattern (ESC 259) 1993 (Dolphin Coins) "FDC"				£5000
1821	437,976 SECVNDO	£10	£30	£150/£200	£400/£600
1821	Noted 1994 --- "Virtually FDC"				£750
1821	SECVNDO proof --- (1989)				£2250
1821	Error TERTIO proof --- --- (1989)				£3300
1822	124,929 SECVNDO	£15	£60	£350	£700/£1200
1822	SECVNDO proof --- --- (1986)				£2500
1822	TERTIO	£14	£70	£250	£650/£900
1822	TERTIO proof --- --- (1986)				£2300
1823	Without edge number, proof only (offers to buy £6000)				
	Bare Head · Shield Reverse				
1825	(ESC 255) BARE HEAD pattern --- (1981)				£3800
1826	(ESC 257) SEPTIMO proof from the sets (1987)				£3000
1828	Pattern in Germanic style (1983) £400				-----

Date	Mintage		Fine	V.F.	E.F.	Abt. Unc/FDC
WILLIAM IV						
	MANTLE design as halfcrown				SILVER 38mm	
1831	W.W.	(ESC 271) (near FDC, minor defects, Seaby £2750)				
1831	W.W.	Proof in gold (collected as £5 pieces)				/£7500
1831	W.Wyon (ESC 273)		---	---	£3000	/£4500
1832	Lead Pattern, extreme rarity edge TERTIO £2000					
1834	A plain edged proof		---	---	---	/£6500
VICTORIA	*YOUNG HEAD*				SILVER 38mm	
1837	Incuse Pattern			Auction (1987)		£2600
1837	Pattern, lead, mirror image (Spink 1988) £650					----
1839	Proofs from the sets (ESC 279)			£800	£1200/£2000	
1844	94,248 Edge VIII :					
	Star-shaped edge stops £10		£40	£250	£750/£1000	
1844	Proof with star-shaped edge stops		---	----		/£4000
1844	Cinquefoil (five leaves) stops		£50	£400	£1200/£1600	
1845	159,192 Edge VIII		£10	£45	£350	£750/£1000
1846	Pattern by W.Wyon (ESC 341)		---	(1980)		/£3000
1847	140,976 Edge XI		£16	£70	£360	£750/£1000
1847	8,000 UNDECIMO proof GOTHIC £560			£1000/£1500		
1847	"Superb example ..... practically as struck" Glendinings '92 £1705					
1847	Noted (2 in gold, Spink-Taisei 1988) the pair £113,000					
1847	Error edge SEPTIMO proof GOTHIC		----		-----	
1847	Without edge number (ESC 291)			£1200/£1600		
1853	460 D.SEPTIMO from the sets £2000			£3000/£4000		
1853	"Magnificent Gem FDC" Whiteaves-Scott '93					£4250
1853	Without edge number (ESC 294)		----	£4500/£6000		
1879	Return to Young Head. Offers for this exceed					£15,000

SILVER 38mm

Reverse: ST. GEORGE and THE DRAGON

Date	Mintage		Fine	V.F.	E.F.	abt Unc/FDC
VICTORIA	Jubilee Head					GOLDEN JUBILEE
1887	173,581		£5	£10	£25	£40/ £60
1887	1,084	proofs	--	---	£150	£250/£325
1888	131,899	close date	£7	£21	£40	£65/£110
1888		wider date	£8	£25	£60	£125/----
1889	1,807,223		£5	£10	£25	£45/ £65
1890	997,862		£7	£18	£40	£65/ £95
1891	566,394		£7	£18	£40	£65/ £95
1892	451,334		£8	£22	£60	£100/£145

Prices asked often have wide variations, for example:
1887 ABU £24; BU £40; BU Gem £50; FDC £75.

Date	Mintage		Fine	V.F.	E.F.	abt Unc/FDC
VICTORIA	Old, Veiled or Widow Head					
1893	1,312	LVI proofs from the sets		£150	£275/£375	
1893	497,845	LVI	£5	£20	£45	£95/£145
1893		LVII	£10	£25	£75	£165/£250
1894	144,906	LVII	£6	£30	£90	£175/----
1894		LVIII	£6	£20	£80	£160/----
1895	252,862	LVIII	£6	£20	£80	£150/----
1895		LIX	£6	£20	£80	£150/----
1896	317,599	LIX	£8	£25	£125	£250/£375
1896		LX	£6	£20	£60	£80/£150
1897	262,118	LX	£6	£20	£60	£80/£150
1897		LXI	£5	£18	£55	£75/£145
1898	161,450	LXI	£10	£30	£90	£180/£275
1898		LXII	£6	£20	£60	£120/£180
1899	166,300	LXII	£6	£20	£60	£120/£180
1899		LXIII	£6	£20	£60	£120/£180
1900	353,356	LXIII	£5	£18	£45	£90/£130
1900		LXIV	£5	£18	£45	£90/£130

Reverse: ST. GEORGE and THE DRAGON abt

Date	Mintage	Fine	V.F.	E.F.	Unc/FDC

EDWARD VII

1902	256,020	£15	£25	£50	£75/£100
1902	15,123 proofs having a matt surface			£65	£85/£110
1902 ★	Pattern	depicting Edward VII, robed, and on horseback			
1902	Pattern	similar to the previous entry, struck in gold			
★	1902 Style as Charles I "Tower" Crown (Spinks 1985) £2,500				

GEORGE V *debased silver of .500 fineness from 1927*

1910	Pattern:		flowing interpretation George/Dragon		
1910	Similar but date in exergue reverse (ESC 389) £3,500				
1927	15,030 proofs from the sets	---		£60	£90/£100
1928	9,034	£20	£40	£70	£95/£160
1928	Noted (1991)	(J.Welsh Gem BU/FDC)			£150
1929	4,994	£25	£50	£90	£150/£225
1930	4,847	£25	£50	£90	£150/£225
1931	4,056	£30	£60	£120	£165/£290
1932	2,395	£40	£65	£140	£200/£300
1932	4 proofs	One noted	GEF/FDC (1986)		£950
1933	7,132	£30	£50	£90	£125/£225
1934	932	£250	£450	£750	£900/£1500
1934	8 proofs	as far back as 1976			£875
1935	714,769 incuse edge lettering			£5	£9/£14
1935	Superior strikings, in special box		---		£20/£30
1935	2,500 silver proofs, raised edge lettering				£200/£250
1935 ★	Some; both incuse and raised, have edge lettering error				
1935 ★★	30 proofs struck in gold	---	---		£7750
1935	A few .925 proofs incuse edge lettering				£1750
1935	A pattern - date in front of horse's head				----
1936	2,473	£40	£70	£140	£225/£275
1936	3 or 4 proofs are thought to exist				----

★ correct order of words: DECUS ET TUTAMEN ANNO REGNI

★★ gold proofs have raised edge lettering

EDWARD VIII

			.500 fine silver		38 mm
1936	Unofficial patterns	---	---	FDC	£20
1936	Noted 1993	---	---	"abt FDC"	£15
1937	designs similar to those of George VI				

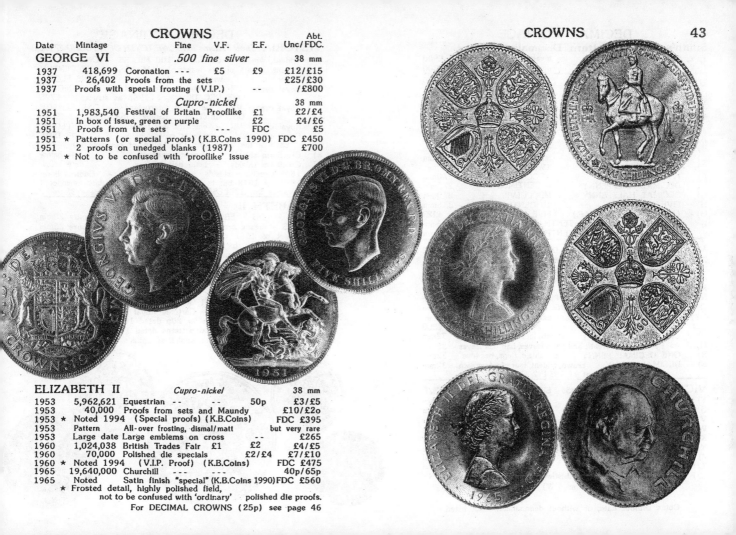

CROWNS

GEORGE VI   *.500 fine silver*   38 mm

Date	Mintage		Fine	V.F.	E.F.	Abt. Unc/FDC.
1937	418,699	Coronation	- - -	£5	£9	£12/£15
1937	26,402	Proofs from the sets				£25/£30
1937		Proofs with special frosting (V.I.P.)		- -		/£800

Cupro-nickel   38 mm

Date	Mintage		Fine	V.F.	E.F.	Abt. Unc/FDC.
1951	1,983,540	Festival of Britain Prooflike	£1			£2/£4
1951		In box of issue, green or purple	£2			£4/£6
1951		Proofs from the sets	- - -		FDC	£5
1951	★	Patterns (or special proofs) (K.B.Coins 1990)			FDC	£450
1951		2 proofs on unedged blanks (1987)				£700

★ Not to be confused with 'prooflike' issue

ELIZABETH II   *Cupro-nickel*   38 mm

Date	Mintage		Fine	V.F.	E.F.	Abt. Unc/FDC.
1953	5,962,621	Equestrian	- -	- -	50p	£3/£5
1953	40,000	Proofs from sets and Maundy			£10/£2o	
1953	★	Noted 1994 (Special proofs) (K.B.Coins)			FDC £395	
1953		Pattern All-over frosting, dismal/matt			but very rare	
1953		Large date Large emblems on cross		- -	£265	
1960	1,024,038	British Trades Fair £1	£2		£4/£5	
1960	70,000	Polished die specials	£2/£4		£7/£10	
1960	★	Noted 1994 (V.I.P. Proof) (K.B.Coins)			FDC £475	
1965	19,640,000	Churchill	- - -	- - -	40p/65p	
1965		Noted Satin finish "special" (K.B.Coins 1990)		FDC £560		

★ Frosted detail, highly polished field,
not to be confused with 'ordinary' polished die proofs.

For DECIMAL CROWNS (25p) see page 46

Smith's Private Pattern Decimals

1, 2, 5 and 10 cents	inverted reverse	£900
1, 2, 5 and 10 cents restrikes	upright reverse	£300

VICTORIA

DECIMAL 'FARTHING' of 1854	1/1000 of £1	a MILLE

1854 Noted 1994 "As struck" MODEL MILLE, GOTHIC HEAD, £125

VICTORIA PATTERNS of 1857   BRITANNIA Reverse   BRONZE

	Legend above Britannia:	Legend below Britannia:	
A)	ONE CENT	MDCCCLVII	16.5mm
B)	HALF FARTHING	ONE CENTIME	17.0mm
C)	TWO CENTS	MDCCCLVII	22.0mm
D)	ONE FARTHING	TWO CENTIMES	22.0mm
E)	FIVE CENTS	MDCCCLVII	27.0mm
F)	DECIMAL HALFPENNY	5 CENTIMES	27.5mm
G)	DECIMAL HALFPENNY	MDCCCLVII	27.0mm
H)	FIVE FARTHINGS	10 CENTIMES	33.5mm
H)	(Noted 1989 about V.F.)	FIVE FARTHINGS	£125
I)	DECIMAL PENNY	ONE TENTH OF A SHILLING	32.5mm
J)	TEN CENTS	ONE TENTH OF A SHILLING	32.5mm

VICTORIA PATTERNS of 1859   DATE BELOW HEAD   BRONZE

K)	HALF DECIMAL PENNY	in wreath oak leaves/acorns	27mm
L)	HALF DECIMAL PENNY	ONE TWENTIETH SHILLING	27mm
M)	ONE DECIMAL PENNY	in wreath oak leaves/acorns	32mm
M)	(Noted 1986 E.F.)	Cupro-nickel and tin	£400
N)	ONE TENTH OF DECIMAL PENNY	A SHILLING	32mm
O)	★ DECIMAL PENNY ★	ONE TENTH OF A SHILLING	32mm
O2)	Has larger lettering and date between ornaments		32mm
O2)	(Noted 1986 E.F.)	Nickel-bronze	£250
P)	ONE DECIMAL PENNY	wreath laurel leaves/berries	32mm
Q)	As P)	but wreath half palm leaves, half oak leaves	32mm
R)	ONE DECIMAL PENNY	lion, shield, flags, bee-hive	32mm
S)	DECIMAL PENNY	crown, trident, laurel/oak wreath	32mm
	See trident of 1961 2 CENTS		

VICTORIA PATTERNS of 1859   SIZE REDUCED   BRONZE

T)	DECIMAL HALF PENNY	laurel wreath with berries	
U)	DECIMAL HALF PENNY	half laurel, half oak, crown	
V)	DECIMAL HALF PENNY	complete circle of palm leaves	
W)	ONE DECIMAL PENNY in exergue	lion and palm tree	
X)	DECIMAL 1 PENNY	below large trident with dolphins	
Y)	ONE PENNY	Una and the Lion DECIMAL in exergue	
Z)	ONE DECIMAL PENNY	wreath alternating oak & laurel	
Z2)	ONE DECIMAL PENNY	wreath half oak, half laurel	
Z3)	Circle of roses, shamrocks, thistles around ONE DECIMAL PENNY		

First three 19.5 mm;   W) to Z3) 27 mm.

Coins without date, or without denomination, not listed.

DECIMAL COINAGE

VICTORIA *Silver Patterns 1848 ONE TENTH OF A POUND 27 mm*

1)	Trident, wreath of oak leaves, 100 MILLES	-	ONE DECADE	
2)	Trident, wreath of oak leaves, 100 MILLES	-	ONE CENTUM	
3)	Trident	- wreath of oak leaves	-	ONE FLORIN
4)	Royal cypher VR	- emblems intertwined	-	ONE DECADE
4)		ONE DECADE (1988 as struck)	£725	
5)	Royal cypher VR	- emblems intertwined	-	ONE CENTUM
5)		ONE CENTUM (Spink 1988 GEF)	£695	
6)	Royal cypher VR	- emblems intertwined	-	ONE FLORIN
7)	Cruciform shields	- rose at centre, below	-	ONE DIME
	Each of the seven with three different obverses (!)			
8)	Cruciform shields	- laureate head	-	date below
9)	Cruciform shields	- plain hair binding	-	date below
10)	1848 Cruciform shields	- crowned bust	-	Godless florin
11)	1851 As 1848 but in Gothic style:	the date as mdcccli		

Values for GODLESS and GOTHIC florins on page 33

ELIZABETH II   *Decimal Patterns*

1 CENT - 1961 - ER - ONE DECIMAL PENNY - Bronze 20mm
2 CENTS - crown, ornamented trident - 1961 - Bronze 25mm
(1986 set of 1961 comprising 1, 2, 5, 10, 20 and 50 cents
sold at Sotheby's for £2,400 plus buyers premium and VAT)

Aluminium quarter penny	- Tudor Rose over 1/4 -	20mm
Bronze half penny	- Welsh Dragon over 1/2 -	17mm
Bronze penny	- Scottish Lion, St Andrews Cross -	20mm
Bronze two pence	- Britannia over large 2 -	26mm
Cupro-nickel five pence	- Three Crowns over 5 -	23mm
Cupro-nickel ten pence	- St George and The Dragon -	28mm
Cupro-nickel twenty pence	- Gartered Royal Arms -	36mm

(in 1982, a decimal pattern for 20p dated 1963   @   £1,500)
(in 1986, full set of decimal patterns dated 1963   @   £4,500)
(in 1986, uniface set artist's copies at Spink's   @   £900)

DECIMAL COINAGE
IN 1982 THE WORD 'NEW' WAS DISCONTINUED
ELIZABETH II

Half New Penny

BRONZE 17mm — THE ROYAL CROWN

Year	Selected	Unc/Proof	Year	Unc/Proof	Year	Selected	Unc/Proof
1971	1,394,188,250	15p/£2	1976	50p/£1	1981		60p/£1
1972	Proof ex-set	---/£3	1977	20p/£1	1982		15p/£1
1973	365,680,000	50p/£1	1978	25p/£2	1983	7,600,000	25p/£1
1974	365,448,000	50p/£1	1979	20p/£2	1984	158,820	£1/£2
1975	197,600,000	50p/£1	1980	30p/£1	Demonetized 31/12/84		

One New Penny

BRONZE 20mm — A PORTCULLIS WITH CHAINS ROYALLY CROWNED

Year	Selected	Unc/Proof	Year	Unc/Proof	Year	Unc/Proof
1971	1,521,666,250	15p/£1	1981	60p/£1	1990	10p/£2
1972		---/£2	1982	40p/£1	1991	10p/£2
1973	280,196,000	50p/£1	1983	50p/£1	1992	10p/£2
1974	330,892,000	60p/£1	1984	20p/£1	1993	....
1975	221,604,000	60p/£1	1985	20p/£1	1994	....
1976	241,800,000	50p/£1	1986	25p/£1	1995	....
1977		---/£1	1986	25p/£1		
1978		---/£2	1987	10p/£1		
1979		25p/£2	1988	15p/£1		
1980		25p/£2	1989	10p/£2		

Two New Pence

BRONZE 26mm — THE BADGE OF THE PRINCE OF WALES

Year	Selected	Unc/Proof	Year	Unc/Proof	Year	Unc/Proof
1971	1,454,856,250	15p/£1	1981	30p/£1.5	1988	20p/£1.5
1972, 1973, 1974		---/£1	1982	£2/£4	1989	20p/£1
1975	144,406,000	75p/£1	1983	£2/£4	1990	15p/£2
1976	135,772,000	75p/£1	1983 ★ with old rev.		1991	15p/£2
1977		25p/£1	1984	£1/£2	1992	15p/£2
1978		£1/£2	1985	20p/£1	1993	....
1979	408,527,000	30p/£2	1986	20p/£1	1994	....
1980		25p/£1	1987	20p/£1.5	1995	....

1983 ★ two authenticated examples, so far, still inscribed 'NEW'.
1985 New MAKLOUF PORTRAIT of The Queen (see page 25)
1992 The twopence became "magnetic" being copper-plated steel.

FIVE PENCE — A THISTLE ROYALLY CROWNED

CUPRO-NICKEL 23mm

Year	Selected	Unc/Proof	Year	Unc/Proof	Notes
1968	98,868,250	50p/--	1981	---/£2	SMALLER 18mm COIN 20p/£2
1969	119,270,000	75p/--	1982	£2/£4	1990 35,000 silver pairs
1970	225,948,525	75p/--	1983	£1/£2	of both sizes £24.50
1971	81,783,475	75p/£2	1984	£1/£2	1990 20,000 silver
1972, 1973, 1974		---/£2	1985	£1/£2	Piedfort £28.95
1975	86,550,000	50p/£2	1986	£1/£2	1991 20p/£2
1976		---/£2	1987	50p/£2	1992 20p/£2
1977		35p/£2	1988	50p/£2	1993 ....
1978	61,000,000	£4/£5	1989	40p/£2	1994 ....
1979		40p/£3	1990	£2/£3	1995 ....
1980		30p/£2			

TEN PENCE — A LION PASSANT GUARDANT ROYALLY CROWNED

CUPRO-NICKEL 28.5mm

Year	Selected	Unc/Proof	Year	Unc/Proof	Notes
1968	336,143,250	60p/--	1978	---/£3	1988 £2/£3
1969	314,008,000	60p/--	1979	£1/£3	1989 £2/£3
1970	133,571,000	£2/--	1980	£1/£3	1990 £2/£5
1971	63,205,000	£1/£3	1981	£1/£3	1991 £3/£5
1972		---/£5	1982	£3/£5	1992 50p/£2
1973	152,174,000	£1/£3	1983	£1/£3	SMALLER 24.5mm 50p/£2
1974	92,741,000	£2/£4	1984	£1/£3	1982 Silver Proof 'pair'
1975	181,559,000	£1/£3	1985	£1/£3	of both sizes £29.95
1976	228,220,000	£1/£3	1986	£1/£3	1993 ....
1977	59,323,000	£1/£3	1987	£2/£3	1994 ....

The florin/two shilling/28.5mm tenpence piece was demonetized 30/6/93.

TWENTY PENCE — A DOUBLE ROSE ROYALLY CROWNED

CUPRO-NICKEL 21.4mm

Year	Selected	Unc/Proof	Year	Selected	Unc/Proof
1982	740,815,000	50p/£6	1989	109,128,890	45p/£4
1982	25,000 silver Piedfort	--/£34	1990		50p/£5
1983	158,463,000	50p/£5	1991		50p/£5
1984	65,350,965	75p/£5	1992		....
1985	74,273,699	50p/£5	1993		....
1986		£1/£5	1994		....
1987	137,450,000	75p/£5	1995		....
1988	38,038,344	45p/£4			

TWENTYFIVE PENCE   38mm

CUPRO-NICKEL CURRENCY :		Proof from Selected Unc/Sets	.925 SILVER PROOF :	F.D.C. from/to
1972	7,452,100 Silver Wedding	65p/£4	100,000	£12/£18
1977	36,989,000 Silver Jubilee	60p/£4	377,000	£9/£12
1977	Selected coin in R.M. folder	£2/--		
1980	Queen Mother's 80th Birthday: 9,477,513	60p/--	83,672	£20/£30
1980	Selected coin in R.M. folder	£1/--		
1981	27,360,279 Royal Wedding	£1/--	218,142	£15/£25
1981	Selected coin in R.M. folder	£1/--		
1989	FOUR-CROWN-COLLECTION of the four silver proofs £125			

(The Case, Booklet and Certificate are, probably, vital to the valuation of this group of coins : see Individual values).

FIFTY PENCE   CUPRO-NICKEL 30 mm

Proofs, are those taken from the sets. They also exist for unlisted dates.

	Selected Unc/Proof		Sel.Unc/Proof		Sel.Unc/Proof
1969	188,400,000 £2/£4	1980	£2/£4	1988	£3/£5
1970	19,461,000 £2/£4	1981	£2/£4	1989	£3/£5
1973	★ 89,775,000 £2/--	1982	£2/£5	1990	£3/£6
Proofs	★ 356,616 cased £4	1983	£2/£5	1991	£3/£6
1976	28,100,000 £2/£4	1984	£2/£5	1992	/£5
1977	£2/£4	1985	£2/£5	1992/93	★★ /£5
1978	£2/£4	1986	£2/£5	★★ Silver	£24
1979	£2/£4	1987	£2/£5	★★ Piedfort	£45
				★★ Gold	£375

★ EEC Commemoratives (also a few V.I.P piedforts)
★★ New design to commemmorate Britain's Presidency/Council of Ministers
1994 "D-Day" in folder £2 · Silver Proof £24 · Piedfort £45 · Gold £375

ONE POUND (One Hundred Pence)

Pale-yellow mixture of metals - 22.5 mm dia. - 3.1 mm thick
has grained (milled) edge, with incuse (struck in) lettering.
England and Northern Ireland variants read: DECUS ET TUTAMEN
(An Ornament and a Safeguard) first used to prevent the "clipping" of coins
Scotland: NEMO ME IMPUNE LACESSIT (No One Provokes Me with Impunity)
For Wales: PLEIDOL WYF I'M GWLAD (True Am I to My Country)

Date	Mintage		Unc./Proof
1983	434,000,000	Royal Coat of Arms general issue	£2/£5
1983	484,900	Selected general issue in wallet	£3/--
1983	50,000	Sterling silver (.925) proofs	£20
1983	10,000	Silver Piedfort proofs.	£110
1984	110,000,000	Thistle for Scotland general issue	£1/£2
1984	27,960	Selected general issue in wallet	£3/--
1984	44,855	Sterling silver (.925) proofs	£22
1984	15,000	Silver Piedfort proofs.	£50
1985	178,000,000	Leek for Wales general issue	£2/£5
1985		Selected general issue in wallet	£3/--
1985	50,000	Sterling silver (.925) proofs	£22
1985	15,000	Silver Piedfort proofs.	£50

DECIMAL COINAGE

One Pound

continued from previous page

		Issue Price Unc.	Proofs from Sets
1986 Not revealed	Flax Plant for Northern Ireland	£1	£3
	Selected general issue in wallet	£2.60	---
1986 50,000	Sterling silver (.925) proofs	£19.95	---
1986 15,000	Silver Piedfort proofs	£38.50	---
1987	An Oak Tree for general issue	£1	£3
	Selected general issue in wallet	£2.75	---
1987 50,000	Sterling silver (.925) proofs	£19.95	---
1987 15,000	Silver Piedfort proofs.	£38.50	---
1988	The Royal Arms of H.M. The Queen (Derek Gorringe)	£1	£3
	Selected general issue in wallet	£2.75	---
1988 50,000	Sterling silver (.925) proofs	£19.95	---
1988 15,000	Silver Piedfort proofs.	£39.50	---
1989	Re-appearance of the Thistle Pound	£1	£3
1989 25,000	Sterling silver (.925) proofs	£19.95	---
1989 10,000	Silver Piedfort proofs.	£39.50	---
1990	Re-appearance of the Leek Pound	£1	£3
1990 25,000	Sterling silver (.925) proofs	£21.25	---
1991	Re-appearance of the Flax Pound	£1	£3
1991 25,000	Sterling silver (.925) proofs	£22.50	---
1992	General Issue (Oak Tree)	£1	£3
1992 25,000	Sterling silver (.925) proofs	£23.50	---
1993	General Issue · Royal Arms	£1	£3
1993 25,000	Sterling silver (.925) proofs	£23.50	---
1993 12,500	Silver Peidfort proofs	£44.50	---
1994	First of New Series (sets only to date)	Unc.	Proof
	Scottish Lion Rampant taken from sets	£3	£6

TWO POUNDS   28.4 mm

Issue Price or Uncirc. Values

1986 COMMEMORATING EDINBURGH COMMONWEALTH GAMES

	Thistle, Wreath, Cross of St.Andrew	£2	Selected in wallet	£4
125,000	Nickel-brass proofs in sets	--	125,000 .500 silver	£14
75,000	925 silver proofs	£25	15,000 gold proofs	£280

1989 COMMEMORATING 300th ANNIVERSARY BILL OF RIGHTS

William & Mary. Not for general issue, but still legal tender.

Bill of Rights	£2	Selected in wallet	£3.95
Claim of Right	£2	Selected in wallet	£3.95
Pair, as picture, loose, but of selected quality			£6.50
Pair, as picture, selected, in Official blister-pack			£7.25
25,000 each Bill and Claim proofs in silver singles			£22.50
Included above: Bill AND Claim proofs in silver sold as a pair			£42.50
10,000 pairs Bill AND Claim proofs, silver, piedfort, pairs			£77.50

1994 COMMEMORATING TERCENTENARY of THE BANK OF ENGLAND

Edge: SIC VOS NON VOBIS (Thus you labour but not for yourselves)
Blister-pack £3.95 · Silver proof £24.50
Gold 'TWO POUNDS' and error not showing value · offers for either £325

FIVE POUNDS ('Crown')   38.61mm

1990 COMMEMORATING THE QUEEN MOTHER's 90th BIRTHDAY

Interlaced Es - Rose and Thistle - Legal Tender £5

	Selected cupro-nickel in official blister-pack issued @		£8.95
150,000	Proofs in Sterling Silver	Issued @	£28.75
2,500	Proofs in 22 carat Gold	Issued @	£625.00

1993   THE CORONATION ANNIVERSARY 1953/1993

Queen's 1953 portrait encircled by mounted trumpeters/swords/sceptres

	Selected cupro-nickel in official blister-pack issued @		£8.95
100,000	Proofs in Sterling Silver	Issued @	£29.50
2,500	Proofs in 22 carat Gold	Issued @	£625.00

PROOF SETS

F. D. C.
from / to

GEORGE IV
1826   140 sets (11) Farthing to five pounds   £17,000/£20,000

WILLIAM IV
1831   145 sets (14) Maundy replaces £5   £12,500/£18,000
    Silver only (8) (Spink 1988) E.F. £4,400   ------

VICTORIA
1839   300 sets (15) In spade shaped case which includes:
     the Una-and-The-Lion gold £5   £22,000/£26,000
1853   460 (16) Quarter-farthing to Gothic 5/-   £18,000/£22,000
1887   797 sets (11) unofficial cases 3d to £5   £4,500/ £6,000
1887   287 sets   3d to 5/-   £600/ £800
1893   773 sets (10) rarely intact 3d to £5   £4,500/£6,500
1893   Short set of six silver coins 3d to 5/-   £800/ £1,000

EDWARD VII
1902   8,066 sets (13) Maundy 1d to £5 (matt)   £1,000/ £1,500
1902   7,057 sets (11) Maundy 1d to sovereign   £350/ £500

GEORGE V
1911   2,812 sets (12) Maundy 1d to £5   £2,000/ £2,500
1911   952 sets (10) Maundy 1d to sovereign   £600/ £750
1911   2,241 sets (8) Maundy penny to half-crown   £200/ £325
1927   15,030 sets (6) 3d to crown   £185/ £250

GEORGE VI
1937   5,501 sets (4) Half-sovereign to £5   £1,200/ £1,500
1937   26,402 sets (15) Farthing to crown + Maundy   £90/ £120
1950   17,513 sets (9) Farthing to half-crown   £30/ £45
1951   20,000 sets (10) Farthing to crown   £40/ £55

ELIZABETH II
1953   40,000 sets (10) Farthing to crown (5/-)   £30/ £42
1953   ★ A large number of sets in plastic wallet (9)   £8/ £9
1968   Decimal souvenir sets, mixed dates in folder   £1
1970   750,000 Last Sterling ½d to 2/6d + medallion   £8/ £12

★ non-proof, selected currency coins
1953 "plastic" sets sometimes (rarely) found with 1/4d Obverse 1 / Reverse B and must, therefore, be at least as rare as that coin (see page 7)

DECIMAL PROOF and Uncirculated SETS

★ = plus Royal Mint medallion   **F.D.C.** from/ to

1971   350,000 (6) ★ half to 50p   £10/£12
1972   150,000 (7) ★ plus Crown   £10/£12
1973   100,000 (6) ★ half to EEC 50p   £7/ £9
1974   100,000 (6) ★ half to 50p   £6/£10
1975   100,000 (6) ★ half to 50p   £7/ £9
1976   100,000 (6) ★ half to 50p   £7/ £9
1977   193,000 (7) ★ Jubilee Crown   £10/£14
1978   88,100 (6) ★ half to 50p   £12/£16
1979   81,000 (6) ★ half to 50p   £12/£18
1980   10,000 (4) half-sov to £5   £850
1980   143,400 (6) ★ half to 50p   £5/£10
1981   5,000 (9) ½p to gold £5   £600
1981   2,500 (2) crown & sov.   £90/£140
1981   100,300 (6) ★ half to 50p   £5/£10
1982   2,500 (4) half-sov to £5   £800
1982   106,800 (7) ★ plus new 20p   £5/£10
1982   205,000 (7) Uncirc in folder   £3/ £5
1983   12,500 (3) ½ sov, sov, £2   £300
1983   107,800 (8) ★ plus 20p & £1   £8/£14
1983   637,100 (8) Uncirc in folder   £5/ £6
1984   7,095 (3) ½ sov, sov, £5   £600
1984   125,000 (8) ★ Scottish £1   £8/£14
1984   158,820 (8) Uncirc in folder   £5/ £6

ISSUE PRICE

1985   125,000 (7) ★ 1p to Welsh £1 Maklouf portrait, blue leatherette case   £18.75
    de-luxe red leather case   £25.75
1985   (7) Uncirc in folder   £4.75
1986   125,000 (8) ★ N.I. £1 & C/wealth £2,
    in blue leatherette case   £21.25
    in de-luxe red leather case   £28.25
1986   (8) Uncirc in folder   £7.95
1987   125,000 (7) ★ 1p to English Oak £1
    in blue leatherette case   £18.95
    in de-luxe red leather case   £25.95
1987   (7) Uncirc in folder   £5.25
1988   125,000 (7) ★ 1p to Royal Arms £1
    in blue leatherette case   £18.95
    in de-luxe red leather case   £25.95
1988   (7) Uncirc in folder   £5.25
1989   125,000 (8) ★ 1p to 'Orange' £2 x 2
    in blue leatherette case   £22.95
    in de-luxe red leather case   £29.95
1989   (8) Uncirc in folder   £5.75
1989   Boy/Girl Baby Packs in Blue/Pink
    either @   £9.95

★ = plus Royal Mint medallion   **F.D.C.** ISSUE PRICE

1990   100,000 (8) ★ 1p, (both 5p),
    50p to Welsh £1
    in blue leatherette case   £21.95
    in de-luxe red leather case   £28.95
1990   (8) Uncirc in folder   £6.25
1990   Boy/Girl Baby Packs in Blue/Pink
    either @   £9.95
1991   100,000 (7) ★ 1p to N.I. £1
    in blue leatherette case   £23.50
    in de-luxe red leather case   £30.60
1991   (8) Uncirc in folder   £7.10
1991   Baby Packs   £11.20
1991   L.s.d. set (dated 1967)   £14.25
1992   100,000 (9) ★ 1p, (10p x 2), (50p x 2) to £1
    in blue leatherette case   £27.50
    in de-luxe red leather case   £34.50
1992   (9) uncirc in folder   £8.75
1992   Baby Packs   £13.95
1992   Wedding Pack   £13.95
1993   100,000 (8) ★ 1p to £5
1993   in blue leatherette case   £28.75
1993   in de-luxe red leather case   £35.50
1993   (8) uncirc 1p to £1 (50p x 2)   £8.75
1993   Baby Gift Set   £13.95
1993   Wedding Collection   £16.50
1994   100,000 (8) ★ 1p to £1
1994   in blue leatherette case   £24.75
1994   in de-luxe red leather case   £32.50
1994   (8) uncirc in folder   £8.75
1994   Baby Gift Set   £13.95
1994   Wedding Collection   £14.95
1995   100,000 ( ) ★ 1p to £1
1995   in blue leatherette case   ------
1995   in de-luxe red leather case   ------
1995   ( ) uncirc in folder   ------
1995   Baby Gift Set   ------
1995   Wedding Collection   ------